"*The Body Image Workbook for Teens* gives girls indispensable tools to develop a positive body image. But, just as importantly, the exercises help girls develop important critical thinking skills. The book is compassionate, direct, and gives girls the opportunity to do what's best for themselves. I can't wait to use the wisdom in these pages with the girls I work with!"

—**Rosalind Wiseman**, author of *Queen Bees & Wannabes*, the book that inspired the motion picture, *Mean Girls*

"With her expert wisdom and her trustworthy tone, Julia V. Taylor offers a brilliant workbook that naturally guides teen girls to get to know and love their authentic selves. Filled with activities and peer anecdotes, this book helps girls identify the specific steps to confidently navigate the journey toward self-love. This workbook is a refreshingly reliable and relatable resource for teens. It is validating, empowering, and very honestly acknowledges how real these struggles are for girls today. In a world where women and girls are battling a very real confidence crisis, *The Body Image Workbook for Teens* serves as a key part of the solution."

—**Haley Kilpatrick**, founder and CEO of *Girl Talk* and author of *The Drama Years: Real Girls Talk about Surviving Middle School— Bullies, Brands, Body Image, and More*

"When I'm asked to recommend the best curricula for girls, I always turn to Julia V. Taylor's work. There are few educators who understand girls as well as her, and *The Body Image Workbook for Teens* is an exceptional example. In this book, Taylor delves beneath the surface of body image distress to help girls own their strengths and value their bodies for what they are—not what they look like. I highly recommend this much-needed tool and look forward to using it myself."

—**Rachel Simmons**, author of *Odd Girl Out, Odd Girl Speaks Out*, and *The Curse of the Good Girl*

"Finding the right tone to connect with teens about body image and body esteem can be a challenge, but *The Body Image Workbook for Teens* hits the mark. The anecdotes, examples, and exercises are pitched perfectly for a teen audience. They capture day-to-day experiences that can undermine teens' self-confidence and provide clear strategies for navigating esteem minefields. An excellent resource to align professionals with teens. All will benefit from affirming strategies that help you value yourself for who you are, not how you look."

> —**Cynthia Bulik, PhD**, author of *The Woman in the Mirror: How to Stop Confusing What You Look Like with Who You Are*

"Julia V. Taylor's *The Body Image Workbook for Teens* is a much-needed antidote to the negative influence media and cultural messages can have on the psyche of the developing adolescent. Educators, school counselors, therapists, parents, and of course, teens—this is the tool we have been waiting for!"

> —**Lisa Flynn**, founder and director of *ChildLight Yoga* and *Yoga 4 Classrooms*, and author of *Yoga 4 Classrooms Card Deck* and *Yoga for Children: 200+ Yoga Poses, Breathing Exercises, and Meditations for Healthier, Happier, More Resilient Children*

"With the growing need for more tangible, practical discussion around body image and self-esteem, this workbook serves as a much-needed resource for teens, educators, and parents everywhere. With its easy-to-follow nature, rewarding exercises, and real-life examples to work off of, readers will gain insight on how to discover their true feelings and begin the journey toward self-love and acceptance."

> —**Jess Weiner**, self-esteem expert and social messaging strategist

the
body image
workbook
for teens

activities to help girls develop a healthy body image in an image-obsessed world

JULIA V. TAYLOR, MA

Instant Help Books
An Imprint of New Harbinger Publications, Inc.

Publisher's Note

Distributed in Canada by Raincoast Books

Copyright © 2014 by Julia V. Taylor
            Instant Help Books
            An Imprint of New Harbinger Publications, Inc.
            5674 Shattuck Avenue
            Oakland, CA 94609
            www.newharbinger.com

INSTANT HELP, the Clock Logo, and NEW HARBINGER are trademarks of
New Harbinger Publications, Inc.

Cover design by Amy Shoup; Edited by Gretel Hakanson; Acquired by Tesilya Hanauer

Library of Congress Cataloging-in-Publication Data on file

Printed in the United States of America

23   22

15   14   13   12   11   10

contents

Dear Reader:

Being a girl in today's world isn't easy. How you feel about yourself and your body can be terribly complicated. There are many factors that can contribute to an unhealthy body image. Our society is saturated with unrealistic expectations about beauty and weight. You can read an article in a magazine about increasing your self-esteem, only to find the next page plastered with diet ads. It's hypocritical and wildly confusing. In addition, there is a ton of intense pressure on teenagers that stems from many sources. From school to friendships to relationships to family issues, it always seems like a balancing act. Sometimes you lose yourself along the way.

The good news is you have the power and ability to change your relationship with your body. I recently saw a quote that I absolutely love. It reads, "You will find a girl prettier than me, smarter than me, and funnier than me, but you will never find a girl just like me." What an important message to send to girls and women, young and old. It's completely true and a great reminder that it is our differences that make beauty beautiful.

This book is designed to help you understand and overcome your body image woes. You will tackle the wide variety of issues that often contribute to an unhealthy body image in order to gain the self-confidence you need to move forward. Working through the activities in this book might not be easy, but it will be worth it. And you're worth it.

Because at the end of each day, week, month, and year, you have this: your body.

You own it.

Take good care of it.

After all, there is only one you.

Best,

Julia

We humans are capable of complex thought, reason, and the mastery of tools. Yet sometimes in life we are handed a tool whose significance we do not understand. It is not until the clarity of hindsight allows us to finally see the value of the gift we were given.

The Body Image Workbook for Teens is a significant gift to you.

I want you to understand this right now. In this very moment—not one or five or thirteen or forty-one years from now—I want you to feel the value of this tool. I want you to fully understand the power that is in the following pages.

I hold the opinion that our bodies are not miserable places to be. They are the only bodies we have, and they are amazing. Or at least, they can be, if we let them. If we focus on what they can do instead of obsessing over what they look like, I think we'd get a lot more enjoyment out of life.

But that is way too simple an answer. At the end of the day, you and I know there is more that goes into it. We have statistics looming in our brains about one-third of fourth-grade girls being on a diet and three-quarters of seventeen-year-olds not liking their bodies. By the time a girl is a teen, she'll have seen tens of thousands of advertisements telling her exactly how she can achieve the status of "beautiful."

So we know what we're up against, this massive wall of self-doubt and self-hate, created by society and fortified by marketers. This wall could be the catalyst for girls hating their bodies their entire lives, until they are old women and the very best years were wasted wishing for thigh gaps and C cups and straight noses and curly hair. As a society, we discuss pieces of this wall, in indirect and insincere ways, but we fail to talk about it in a way that dismantles it. A way that takes it apart, brick by brick.

Girls need the tools that will allow them to take down that wall, brick by brick, until each manipulation, each insecurity, each beauty myth is strewn about their feet like rubble that now has no sense and no structure. All its parts exposed. Reframed. Rejected.

What you are holding is a tool, and I want you to recognize that in this moment. You are going to turn the page and have the dots connected for you. In *The Body*

Image Workbook for Teens, Julia Taylor explains so well our feelings about our bodies and the difference between a thought, a feeling, and a behavior. And she does so in such a brilliant way, one that decodes the ways girls were taught to think about themselves and provides new thought-loops for them that are full of self-love and self-acceptance.

With respect and understanding for what girls experience today, this workbook lets teens know they are not alone. It doesn't trivialize what they are going through, and it normalizes their struggles. Each activity holds so much potential and power; each script allows the reader to get one step closer to practicing what positive body image looks like and, most importantly, what positive body image feels like.

The Body Image Workbook for Teens contains a complete set of tools to take apart the wall of negative messages piece by piece so that girls learn they are more than the sum of their parts. This workbook is in your hands today, and today is the correct time to recognize the significance of the tool you've been given.

You are more than the sum of your parts.

With love and encouragement,

—Melissa Atkins Wardy
  author of *Redefining Girly: How Parents Can Fight the Stereotyping and Sexualizing of Girlhood, from Birth to Teen*

acknowledgments

This book would not have been possible without the patience, encouragement, support, and sheer fabulousness of New Harbinger Publications Acquisitions Manager Tesilya Hanauer. Tesilya: I am beyond grateful to have you in my corner. Thank you, so very much.

Thank you to my multitalented teen critics, Blair Burnett and Claire Bridges. I appreciate your time, honest feedback, and willingness to have raw conversations about incredibly tough stuff. The insight and wisdom you two possess extends far beyond your years. I look forward to seeing the women you both become.

Finally, I am tremendously thankful to have collaborated with Jan Thrasher, whose understanding of girls is remarkable and inspiring. Jan: Thank you for your contributions to this book. I hope you continue to be a guiding light to young women.

Part 1
All About Body Image
(Activities 1–8)

1 identifying feelings

for you to know

During your teen years, it's common to experience a ton of different feelings within a very short period of time. One minute you may feel fabulous, and the next minute you may feel like crying. To complicate matters, sometimes you don't even know why.

As you begin working on your body image, the term *feelings* is going to come up a lot. A feeling is a temporary emotional state. Feelings come and go and can be completely confusing.

> When it comes to my body, I never know what I feel. It's totally confusing. If someone gives me a compliment, I may feel happy, or I may not believe it and feel suspicious all day long. Or, I can be in a great mood then read a magazine and feel so depressed. Sometimes I am super excited to wear a new outfit, and then I try it on and cry because it looks stupid. I'm all over the place.
>
> —Blair

Thinking about body image will probably bring up a lot of different feelings. Some may be pleasant, and others might be quite uncomfortable—that's OK. The great thing about feelings is that you own them; they are yours. Nobody can dictate how you "should" feel, nor do you need to apologize for feeling a certain way. Recognizing and owning your feelings is an important part of the process of becoming self-aware. Finally, it's also important to identify the wide range of feelings you feel; the ones besides the typical fine, sad, and mad.

for you to explore

A colossal list of feelings appears on pages 5 and 6. You may need to refer to the list as you work your way through this book. For now, read over them and circle all the feelings you have experienced in the last week. When you have finished, choose a few from the pleasant side and a few from the unpleasant side, and write when you felt that way.

For example:

I *felt* peaceful *when* I had the house to myself on Tuesday night.

I *felt* guarded *when* I met a group of new people at school.

Your turn:

I felt ___scared___ when ___I went to my first day of school___.

I felt _____ when _____.

I felt _____ when _____.

I felt _____ when _____.

I felt _____ when _____.

I felt _____ when _____.

I felt _____ when _____.

I felt _____ when _____.

I felt _____ when _____.

I felt _____ when _____.

explore more

Feelings check-in: How are you feeling right now, right this very second? List whatever you feel, and try not to use "fine," "sad," or "mad"—go deeper than that.

_____

_____

_____

_____

_____

_____

_____

Pleasant Feelings

affectionate	eager	inspired	refreshed
alert	ecstatic	interested	rejuvenated
amazed	empowered	intrigued	relaxed
amused	encouraged	invigorated	relieved
animated	energetic	involved	rested
appreciative	engaged	joyful	revived
astonished	enthralled	lively	safe
awed	enthusiastic	loving	satisfied
blissful	excited	mellow	secure
calm	fascinated	moved	surprised
centered	friendly	open	sympathetic
comfortable	fulfilled	optimistic	thankful
compassionate	giddy	passionate	thrilled
confident	glad	peaceful	touched
content	grateful	pleased	warm
curious	happy	proud	
delighted	hopeful	radiant	

Unpleasant Feelings

afraid	disappointed	horrified	regretful
aggravated	disconnected	hostile	resentful
alienated	discouraged	hurt	sad
ambivalent	disgusted	impatient	self-conscious
angry	disturbed	insecure	sensitive
animosity	edgy	irked	shocked
annoyed	embarrassed	jealous	stressed
anxious	enraged	livid	tense
appalled	envious	lonely	terrified
apprehensive	exhausted	miserable	torn
ashamed	flustered	mortified	uncomfortable
baffled	frustrated	nervous	upset
betrayed	furious	numb	vulnerable
confused	guarded	outraged	withdrawn
cranky	guilty	overwhelmed	worried
depleted	heartbroken	panicked	
depressed	hopeless	perturbed	

thoughts, feelings, and behaviors 2

for you to know

Thoughts, feelings, and behaviors all influence one another. Most people have thousands of random, fleeting thoughts each day. If you're struggling with your body image, many of your thoughts and feelings might be about your body. Some of your thoughts will stir up feelings, and some of your thoughts *and* feelings will cause certain behaviors.

You just learned that a feeling is a temporary emotional state. Your thoughts, feelings, and behaviors are all connected. Thoughts are all of the things you think about. *What am I going to have for lunch? She looks angry.* Usually, you *feel* something as a *result* of your thoughts. *Hungry. Concerned.* Finally, a behavior is how you act as a result of your thoughts and feelings. *I had a sandwich for lunch. I asked her if she was OK.* We constantly go through the thoughts, feelings, and behaviors cycle—all are very powerful and can greatly influence our lives.

This morning I woke up really late and didn't have time to get ready. I looked awful: my hair was greasy, my clothes were wrinkled, and I can't even remember if I brushed my teeth. I felt disgusting, and I'm pretty sure that everyone was staring at me thinking what a gross, wrinkled-clothes loser I am. I couldn't concentrate on anything because I felt so self-conscious. So, after first period I went home.

—*Savannah*

Let's examine Savannah's inner dialogue.

Thoughts: *I looked awful: my hair was greasy, my clothes were wrinkled, and I can't even remember if I brushed my teeth.*

Feelings: *I felt disgusting.*

Behavior: *I went home.*

It's important to know that your thoughts and feelings are not always the truth. Chances are if you're working through this book, your feelings, thoughts, and behaviors toward your body aren't always accurate or positive. You may even feel so badly about your body that you miss out on important events that you'd like to be a part of. You can change this.

for you to explore

Read the following situations and answer the questions below each one.

1. You wake up one morning only to discover you broke out. Majorly. That afternoon, you decide to go to a friend's house, and she has two minuscule zits on her face that are barely noticeable, yet she complains about them the whole time you are there.

What would you think? _That's srang I mean you can't evenly see them_

How would you feel? _uncomfortable_

What would you *want* to do? _leave_

What would you *actually* do? _stay and ask her to stop matter and that it doese not_

2. Your two best friends decide to go on a crazy new fad diet, and all they talk about is food, how much they weigh, and the workout they are doing.

What would you think? _?_

How would you feel? _insucer_

What would you *want* to do? _to talk about somthing else_

What would you *actually* do? _go along with it_

9

3. Your mom constantly nags you about how you look and how you dress, and she is starting to make rude comments about what you eat. She says things like "You're not going to wear that, are you?" and "I hate it when you do your hair like that." There are a million more examples. If you tell her to stop, she claims to be "trying to help." You don't want her help.

What would you think? _____ thats ruda _____

How would you feel? _____ vrzut _____

What would you *want* to do? _____ run away _____

What would you *actually* do? _____ to what she says _____

Now, think about a recent situation that impacted how you feel about your body.

What was the situation? _____ ? _____

_____

What were your thoughts? _____ ? _____

_____

How did you feel? _____ ? _____

_____

What did you do as a result of your thoughts and feelings? _____

_____ ? _____

explore more

Read each statement below and circle whether it represents a thought, feeling, or behavior.

1. I'm nervous about the pool party next weekend.   Thought   (Feeling)   Behavior

2. I don't know why she always does that.   (Thought)   Feeling   Behavior

3. I destroyed my room trying to find something to wear.   Thought   Feeling   (Behavior)

4. My life would be better if I didn't look like this.   (Thought)   Feeling   Behavior

5. I left the party.   Thought   Feeling   (Behavior)

6. I am self-conscious about my freckles.   Thought   (Feeling)   Behavior

7. I always break out. ?   (Thought)   Feeling   Behavior

8. I worry about my weight a lot.   (Thought)   Feeling   Behavior

9. I always straighten my curly hair.   Thought   Feeling   (Behavior)

10. I feel ugly after I read a fashion magazine.   (Thought   Feeling)   Behavior

5. Behavior
4. Thought
3. Behavior
2. Thought
1. Feeling

10. Thought
9. Behavior
8. Thought
7. Thought
6. Feeling

3 all about body image

for you to know

Body image, simply put, is how you feel *about* your body and how you feel *in* your body. Body image isn't how you physically look; it's how you *feel* about how you look. Your friends, your peers, your family, your lifestyle, your cultural background, and the media can all impact your body image.

People who have a healthy body image generally

- like their body

- accept their body

- feel confident and comfortable with their body

- don't believe they would be better liked if they looked differently

- don't spend a lot of time focused on their weight or looks

- value who they are, not just what they look like.

For example:

My body is strong, and I am exceptionally tall. I tower over my friends and always look funny in pictures, but funny in a good way. I know girls who spend all their time worrying about what they look like. They wear way too much makeup and talk about how fat they are. I don't do that. I never will. I think I look fine with or without makeup. I mean, I like makeup, but I don't have to wear it to prove something. When I wear clothes that don't fit right, I feel self-conscious. So, I usually just wear what makes me feel good. Some days it's a dress and cute pair of shoes; other days it's yoga pants and a sweatshirt. I don't let my height, clothes, appearance, weight, or what other people think bother me. I have better things to think about.

—Riley

People who have an unhealthy body image may

- obsess negatively over their looks

- worry excessively about how much they weigh

- have an inaccurate perception of what they really look like

- focus and fixate on a part, or parts, of their body they wish looked different

- compare themselves to others and wish they looked like them

- feel insecure and blame it on their body

- believe all their problems would go away if they could change their looks.

For example:

My body is all wrong. My nose is crooked, and my legs are too short. My hair sucks; it's curly and gets frizzy the second I leave the house. I know that I would be more popular if I could lose weight, especially in my stomach. All the popular girls have flat stomachs. I can't wear the clothes I want because I look fat in them. I look fat in everything. I've tried a lot of different ways to lose weight. They don't work. I guess I am just meant to be fat and ugly and unpopular and unhappy. Forever.

—Taryn

Having a healthy body image doesn't mean you don't care about your looks; it means you value and appreciate your body. Body image is all about balance, meaning how you feel about your body doesn't always run the show. A healthy body image gives you the freedom and flexibility to be yourself. It means accepting and appreciating your body for what it is and what it does, not what it looks like. Developing a healthy body image takes time, patience, and hard work—but it's worth it. You're worth it.

for you to explore

Think about the inner dialogue of the girls described above, and take a moment to consider your own body image. Using the examples above as a guide, freewrite your own inner dialogue, voice, or feelings—the things you tell yourself about your body.

_____

_____

_____

_____

_____

_____

Read what you just wrote.

How do you feel about your overall body image? Is it negative and critical? Is it positive and supportive? Or is it a little bit of both?

_____

_____

_____

Do any of your words or phrases repeat themselves? If yes, which ones?

_____

_____

_____

Now, get a highlighter and something else (like a different color pen) to write with. Highlight the words or phrases that feel positive. Now, using a different color than the one you wrote in, underline the negative and self-critical phrases or words.

Looking at your highlights, what do you notice about your body image? Did you notice anything surprising when you looked at your highlighted and underlined words and phrases? Does your overall body image reflect your inner dialogue? Are your thoughts balanced—both negative and positive? Or are they mostly critical?

_____

_____

_____

explore more

Think about why you're reading this book; what do you want to gain from it? Having a few healthy (positive, attainable, forward-thinking) goals will help you stay focused on what you hope to achieve by completing this book.

Below, list at least two healthy goals (you can always write more) that you are willing to try.

For example:

By the end of this book, I want to be able to stop comparing myself to others.

By the end of this book, I want to be able to look in the mirror and notice things about my body that I like.

Your turn:

Goal one: _____

_____

_____

Goal two: _____

_____

_____

your reflection 4

for you to know

The automatic negative thoughts that can be stirred up by a casual glance at your reflection can be endless and exhausting. Understanding, recognizing, and replacing these thoughts will help you turn your attention to the positive.

When you look at your reflection in the mirror, what do you focus on? What are your automatic thoughts? Do you have a particular thing or body part that you fixate on?

Why do I always break out right before something important? It's disgusting. I hate my skin.

I need a nose job. Now.

My knees are bony.

I have zero eyelashes.

Ears. Dumbo. I hate them.

No boobs. Negative A cup.

Fat. Stomach.

I'm so pale. I look like a ghost.

I hate myself.

Do these statements sound familiar? Automatic negative thoughts are instantaneous and have incredible power over how you feel and behave. It doesn't have to be this way. With practice, you can change your focus.

for you to explore

The goal of this activity is for you to reduce automatic self-criticism and to learn to see yourself as you truly are, without judgment. Read carefully—this is a long one!

1. In the chart on the next pages, write the first word or brief thought that comes to mind when you think about your own physical features.

2. Next, label each word or thought as truth or judgment. For example, if your nose is crooked, and you think, *My nose is crooked,* that's the *truth*. If you think, *My nose is ugly, and I need a nose job,* that contains *judgment*.

3. Finally, for each time you wrote "judgment," come up with a replacement word or thought that is positive. A replacement thought is something you're willing to say to yourself to combat judgmental thoughts or to make the truth feel OK to you. If you are having trouble coming up with a nonjudgmental replacement word or thought, think about what that body part does for you. Why *could* you be grateful for it? Even if it's as simple as the mere function of that body part, write it down. It's a start.

Here's an example:

Body Part	Your Word or Thought	Truth or Judgment	Replacement Word or Thought (for judgments)
Hair	*Flat and greasy*	*Judgment*	*Straight*
Calves	*Toned*	*Truth*	*I like my calves.*
Arms	*Freakishly long*	*Judgment*	*They are really long, and I'm self-conscious. But they are my arms. I need them, and I cannot change their length.*

Now, your turn:

Body Part	Your Word or Thought	Truth or Judgment	Replacement Word or Thought (for judgments)
Skin			
Hair			
Eyebrows			
Eyelashes			
Eyes			
Ears			
Nose			
Lips			
Teeth			
Cheeks			

Body Part	Your Word or Thought	Truth or Judgment	Replacement Word or Thought (for judgments)
Chin			
Neck			
Shoulders			
Breasts			
Arms			
Hands			
Nails			
Chest			
Back			
Stomach			
Hips	Fat	Idk	Idk

Body Part	Your Word or Thought	Truth or Judgment	Replacement Word or Thought (for judgments)
Butt			
Thighs			
Knees			
Calves			
Ankles			
Feet			
Toes			
Other belly	fat	idk	idk
Other _____			

Now, cross out all of your judgments, and highlight their replacement word or thought. Read over your replacement words and thoughts, and practice saying each one aloud. It may be difficult. At first, you may not even believe what you're saying. That's OK. The goal is to practice turning your attention first to the truth.

explore more

Using the chart on the previous pages, circle a few of the body parts you scrutinize the most when you look in the mirror. Find sticky notes, washable markers, or even old eyeliner, and write your replacement thoughts about these parts directly onto your mirror. Practice saying them each time you look in the mirror. Each and every time. And remember: it's completely normal to have a bad day now and then. Accept where you are, and keep trying to focus first on *your* truth.

you are more than a body   5

for you to know

Your body is just that: a body. You have important qualities and features and talents that have nothing to do with your appearance. It's easy to focus solely on what you see, on what you actually look like. But the truth is, you are so much more than your looks.

When something is wrong, it is not likely due to the size of your thighs, the length or color of your hair, or the anatomical location of your nose. It probably has more to do with your insecurities than anything else. How you look is not reflective of who you are inside or what you're capable of doing. When you try something that doesn't work and you can't figure out why, it's easy to turn your insecurities into body blaming because your body is right in front of you.

I don't stand a chance of being elected for student-body government. I'm not popular like the other girls. My hair is wrong. My clothes are wrong. My body is wrong. I am wrong.

Instead of blaming your body, it's important to look at the facts and identify your strengths.

I get good grades, have excellent teacher recommendations, and am really good at public speaking. My speech will rock, no matter what. It will suck if I don't win, but I'll deal with it and maybe run again next year.

The reality is you don't always win, and things don't always go as planned. Nobody is perfect. When you are able to step back and grasp reality, you might be able to stop blaming your body.

for you to explore

Read the scenarios below, and consider the differences between the body blaming and the reality of the situation each girl is in.

Body blaming: *I like to run and was thinking about trying out for the cross-country team. Last night, I went running with a girl who was on the team last year. She is way skinnier and faster and a lot taller than me. Now I'm thinking I shouldn't try out.*

Reality: *The girl I ran with is skinnier and faster and taller than me, but that doesn't make me a bad runner.*

Body blaming: *At lunch, my friends commented on how much I ate. I didn't think it was that much. Now they all think that I am a fat loser with no self-control.*

Reality: *They were messing around with me and didn't mean to hurt my feelings. I was having a really bad day. I've made comments about what they eat, and I wasn't serious. I guess I never thought about how it might affect them. Maybe we could talk about other things during lunch.*

Using the examples above as a guide, consider your own body-blaming situations. Think about times that you've linked feelings of insecurity with an external quality like your looks or your size. Dig deep and rewrite each situation to identify the reality.

Your body-blaming situation: _____

_____

Reality: _____

_____

Your body-blaming situation: _I am fat and_

hairg

Reality: _I am myself_

Your body-blaming situation: _____

_____

Reality: _____

_____

explore more

It's important to recognize the many qualities you possess that have nothing to do with how you look.

List three things you love to do (making jewelry, riding horses, playing the piano, etc.):

1. _____

2. _____

3. _____

List three quirky things about you (hilariously clumsy, accidently loud, always fall asleep while watching movies, etc.):

1. _____

2. _____

3. _____

List three important roles you have (daughter, sister, friend, etc.):

1. _____

2. _____

3. _____

Write three positive words your friends or family would use to describe your personality (genuine, caring, strong willed, etc.):

1. _____

2. _____

3. _____

6 befriending your body

for you to know

People often bash their bodies and talk to themselves in ways that they would never talk to their friends or family. The more you do it, the more you believe the things you say.

Part of having a healthy body image is learning to be kind to yourself. Speaking to yourself in an unkind manner only fuels self-criticism and body hatred.

I didn't have time to wash my hair. It looks greasy and stupid. I hate my hair.

My legs look short and fat in all my jeans.

I ate way too much for breakfast. I have no self-control.

I know I failed my test. I am so stupid. I should have studied more. I am worthless.

I probably gained a million pounds last night. I need to go to the gym. Now.

Reread the statements above as if you were saying them to someone else. For example: "You ate way too much for breakfast. You have no self-control." Would you really ever say anything like that directly to a friend or anyone else? Probably not. In order to befriend your body, you have to turn the bashing into compassion.

for you to explore

Think about all the times you've bashed your body. Use the space below to write a heartfelt apology letter to your body for the way you've talked to it. Be creative and specific and genuine. Your body deserves it.

_____

_____

_____

_____

_____

_____

_____

_____

_____

_____

explore more

Now that you've apologized to your body, let's explore some different ways you can treat your body with kindness and compassion. Circle at least three things on the list below that appeal to you, and try them within a week. You can circle as many as you'd like, or come up with other acts of kindness toward yourself and your body.

Take a long walk.

Read your favorite book again.

Bake something.

Sing loudly.

Wear something that makes you feel good.

Take a bubble bath.

Do yoga.

Go to a playground and swing.

Take five minutes to sit in your dark closet and just breathe.

Listen to your favorite song on repeat.

Draw, color, or paint.

Journal.

Play a board game with a young child.

Pick some flowers and put them by your bed.

Other: _____

After you've tried at least three things, write about your experience below.

What activities did you try? _____

_____

How did it feel to take time for yourself? _____

_____

How did it feel to be kind to yourself? _____

_____

Write one thing you will keep doing to practice self-compassion. _____

_____

7 your body biography

for you to know

Your body tells a unique story—its own biography. You are a blend of rich and diverse cultural history. Understanding where your body comes from—and more importantly, *whom* it comes from—can help you appreciate your physical features.

You are more than just your looks; you are a collective masterpiece of genes and memories and experiences that nobody else has. How many times has someone told you that you look like your mother, father, aunt, or cousin, or some other family member? There are probably too many to count!

> *Last summer, I went to a family reunion and met some distant cousins for the first time. It was crazy how similar we looked, and we had never even met! We all have the "family nose," which I used to think was an evil curse, but now I think it's kind of cool since I'm not the only one with it.*
>
> *—Lacy*

Your body is specifically designed for you. But it's easy to get caught up in a trap of wishing and wanting to look like someone else, or comparing your body to unrealistic images that you see all around you. Creating a body biography will help you understand the story of your physical features and help you accept you for you.

for you to explore

Look through family photos, old and new, and try to piece together a history of yourself. Instead of looking at what you *are not*, look at what *you are*. For example: *I never knew my great-grandmother, but I have her eyes. Also, I have huge dimples when I smile, and she did too!*

When you're done, answer the following questions:

What did you first notice about your resemblance to other family members?

_____

_____

Where do your eyes come from? _____

Whose hair do you have? _____

_____

Whose build do you have? _____

_____

Whom do you act like? _____

_____

What parts of you are completely unique? _____

_____

Now, hopefully you understand a little bit about why you look how you look. Let's put it all together and create your own body biography.

First, draw an outline of a body on a plain piece of paper. Now, get color—you can use whatever you'd like: paint, magazines, glue, chalk, crayons, markers. Label each area of your body with family names, memories, and so on. *I am writing my grandmother's name on both of my hands. When I was little, I used to sit in her lap, and she'd tell me that her hands used to look just like mine.*

Fill the outline of your body with memories that have shaped your perception of the world. *When I was younger, I loved to help my mom in the garden. We never wore gloves, and our hands got really dirty. We didn't care about the dirt or the world around us—we just dug and planted and talked and enjoyed each other.*

When you have finished, take a moment to appreciate your work. Let your body biography be a reminder of all the people and experiences that make up who you are. You are more than your looks; you are made up of your history, your memories, and the generations of those who came before you.

explore more

Look closely at your body biography.

What is the memory or part of you that you enjoy the most? _____

_____

Whom does it come from? _____

_____

Write a letter to this person, explaining your connection and what it means to you. If you are able to contact that person, you may want to mail your letter to him or her. Even if you are not able to contact your person, go through the ritual of writing the letter, put it in an envelope, and tuck it away in a special place.

8 point out the positive

for you to know

When you take the time to actually write down the positive truths about your body, it can be powerful. You may think something positive, but writing it down can give more meaning to a thought.

Have you ever heard the phrase "Seeing is believing"? What that basically means is that physical evidence is way more convincing than just hearing something said aloud. Now that you're almost finished with the first section, hopefully you've got a pretty good understanding of your own body image. Continuing to acknowledge the positive truths of your body can help you move forward as you work on developing a healthier body image. This isn't always easy, and it may take a ton of practice. To help you wrap up this section, take the time to reflect and write down what you've learned.

for you to explore

Use the space below to archive ten positive truths about your body—for example, *My body is strong.* Write things you like or love or adore about your body and want to keep focusing on, such as *I feel great when I treat my body with kindness instead of cruelty.* Don't think too hard about this. Just write whatever comes first to your mind.

1. _____

2. _____

3. _____

4. _____

5. _____

6. _____

7. _____

8. _____

9. _____

10. _____

explore more

Take a few minutes to think about the work you put into the last seven activities. Using the space below, freewrite about what the process was like for you. Think about where you were in the beginning versus where you are now. What, if anything, has changed? In what areas have you improved? What areas do you need to work on? What support do you need from others, and how will you gather it? How are you feeling? Be honest with yourself, and keep moving forward.

_____

_____

_____

_____

_____

_____

_____

_____

Part 2
The Realities of Girlhood
(Activities 9–16)

9 changing bodies

for you to know

Dealing with the changes your body goes through during your teenage years is difficult. For some girls, the hardest part is just trying to make sense out of everything. It can be wildly confusing and you may often feel as though nobody understands.

One minute I was a little girl running down the beach without a care in the world. My body was nothing other than my body. The next minute, I was completely self-conscious. I remember it being right around the time I got my first period. When I went in the ocean, I would leave my shorts nearby, always in a hurry to put them on the second I got out of the water. I thought everyone was looking at my ginormous legs, which felt totally out of proportion compared to every other part of my body. It felt so wrong.

—Ava

It starts with puberty. First come the mood swings. Then your whole body shape changes. Just when you think your body is done changing, it changes again. And if that isn't enough, it seems as though everyone notices.

You may feel as if nobody understands. It doesn't feel fair. All this turmoil can wreak havoc on your body image. It's important to recognize that your body is still just that—your body.

for you to explore

Create a body image archive by recording your positive body memories. Recall the times you felt that your body was healthy and strong and you didn't worry about what it looked like. Maybe you were four years old and learned how to climb the old oak tree in your front yard. *My arms and legs were strong and could bend and twist until I got to the tallest branch!* Or maybe in sixth grade your school did a community service project, and you helped build a house. *I carried long pieces of wood back and forth from a truck for hours! It felt awesome to know that my hard work helped a family in need.* Work your way up until now. Remember to consider the things your body did for you, not what it looked like.

For example:

Age: *9*

Positive body memory: *I won a jump rope competition at school.*

Thoughts and feelings: *I thought I was the coolest girl in the world! I remember being so proud of myself. I slept wearing the medal I won for an entire week!*

Your turn:

Age: _____

Positive body memory: _____

_____

Thoughts and feelings: _____

_____

Age: _____

Positive body memory: _____

_____

Thoughts and feelings: _____

_____

Age: _____

Positive body memory: _____

_____

Thoughts and feelings: _____

_____

Each day, try to spend some time reflecting on what your body physically did for you that day. Give yourself permission to appreciate the amazing things it does, instead of focusing on what it looks like.

explore more

Younger children usually think of their bodies as vessels that help them run, play, eat, and think. They generally don't think of body parts with negativity or judgment. As they grow older, something shifts. Like the little girl running on the beach, something may have shifted in you, too.

Think hard: When was the first time you noticed your body was more than "just a body"?

_____

Where were you? _____

_____

Who was with you? _____

_____

What happened? _____

_____

What did it feel like? _____

_____

How did you react? _____

_____

What changed afterward? _____

_____

Compared to then, how do you see your body now? _____

_____

Next, look over what you just wrote, and normalize your experience by talking to another female whom you trust. Almost every woman has experienced this, so you shouldn't have too much trouble finding someone. Read her the beach girl story and ask, "When was your body more than your body?" or any other questions you'd like. Using the space below, write about what she said and how you felt listening to her personal memories.

What were the similarities in your stories? _____

_____

What were the differences? _____

_____

What else did you notice? _____

_____

How did talking to someone else about her body image make you feel?

_____

_____

your realm of control 10

for you to know

It's super easy to feel like you're losing control when you're a teenager. Your body changes rapidly, your mood swings back and forth like a pendulum, friendships go awry, and you are suddenly slapped with decisions you've never had to make before. You want everything to be OK, but it's not—and that's OK.

The past month has sucked. I basically break out every day, which stresses me out, which probably makes me break out more. I have a million things to do and stay up all night and am tired all day. My friends have all been fighting, and I'm always in the middle. I look like a giant marshmallow in everything I wear. My parents are so annoying. My sister gets all the attention, and my brother always needs to be driven somewhere. I'm pretty much invisible.

—Nevaeh

It's easy to go straight to hit the panic button when you're feeling overwhelmed. While things might seem hopeless and daunting and completely out of control, you probably have more control than you think. For example, if you're exhausted because you stay up until midnight or later doing homework, you may need to manage your time differently. This is something in your realm of control. Or if all your friends are fighting and you are in the middle, you can refuse to be involved. It's not easy, but ultimately you control your physical and emotional involvement in that situation. Most of the things you do in life are a choice. When things feel out of control, making the choice to change your thoughts and behaviors can help make things feel manageable.

for you to explore

Think about everything that you currently have going on in your life that feels out of control but is actually manageable. In the chart below, list the things that you feel are out of control on the left and the solutions to regain control on the right. Remember: you don't have control over other people's thoughts, reactions, or feelings—but you have control over your reaction to them.

For example:

Things That Feel Out of Control	How I Can Regain Control
My friends fighting with each other	*Stay out of it, or tell them I don't want to be in the middle*
Not enough time to get everything done	*Prioritize my schedule*

Your turn:

Things That Feel Out of Control	How I Can Regain Control

explore more

Sometimes you will face situations that you simply cannot control, like your face breaking out, the rain ruining your soccer game, or your mom being late—every single day. When this happens, try to recognize and accept your lack of control. Say to yourself, *I have no control over this*. Letting things go that you don't have any control over can be both liberating and empowering.

Balloons are symbolic of both holding on and letting go. Think about the things you have zero control over and need to let go of. Write those things in the balloons below. Say, "Let it go" out loud, take a deep breath, and really try to let it go.

11 fitting in

for you to know

The nagging, internal pressure to fit in is very real. Girls often base their self-worth on the opinions of their friends and peers. This social pressure can create feelings of fear, insecurity, and self-doubt and can cause girls to feel constant pressure to change who they are.

Fitting in might start as something small. You say you agree with something you really don't agree with. Or maybe you pretend you like something you cannot stand. Or it may be something bigger: you wear clothes that you don't really like or change your hair color or talk badly about your body to sound like the girls around you.

All of my friends have perfect bodies. I'd give anything to look like them. They always call me cute. I hate being called cute. Cute means fat. Cute means I'll never have a date. I bought the clothes brands they wear (which, by the way, I don't like), I wear my makeup like they do, and I even highlighted my hair because someone told me that mine looked "mousy." What bothers me the most is they always call other girls fat and make fun of how they look. Nothing is off limits. I mean, they don't do it to their faces, but they do it in front of me, and I am bigger than the girls they make fun of. It makes me hate my body and worry what they say about me when I'm not around. I don't know why I care so much, but I do. I just want to fit in.

—Ella

Fitting in is very different from belonging. When you try to fit in, you change yourself. When you truly belong, you feel comfortable being yourself and are accepted for who you are. Truly belonging means always being honest and never altering yourself for the sake of others' comfort.

I have known the same group of girls forever. There are four of us. We live on the same street, and all our parents are good friends. We've all changed a lot and gone through different phases. We hang out with different people now and are always super busy, but we are still really tight. All of us have gone through so much together, and I know I can always count on them. It's cool because I don't have to worry about what I look like, what I say, or even what problems I have. They accept me, no matter what.

—Claudia

Belonging is pressure-free. It's healthy and natural to experiment with different trends, especially as a teenager. It's also healthy and natural to admire qualities and traits of your friends. But it becomes unhealthy when it *feels* wrong to you; it becomes unhealthy when you lose your real self along the way.

for you to explore

Think about a time when you felt pressure to change yourself to fit in. It might have been with your really good friends, a sports team, or a group of people that you thought was cool and that you wanted to hang out with.

Specifically, what part of yourself did you feel pressure to change?

_____

_____

Describe why you felt as though you needed to change.

_____

_____

What was happening around you that made you feel as if you could not be your true self?

_____

_____

What was happening inside of you? What were the physical messages your body was sending?

_____

_____

Now, honestly consider what would have happened if you had just been *you*.

How do you think the situation would have been different if you had been your true self?

_____

_____

_____

What would you have said or done differently?

_____

_____

What do you think the outcome would have been?

_____

_____

explore more

The desire to fit in and to try out different things is healthy. Fitting in becomes problematic when it requires you to change something you *don't want* to change or to do something you are really *uncomfortable* doing—for example, changing how you dress because you want to look more like the group you are hanging out with. Doing it because you really like their style is completely healthy. However, changing how you dress because someone told you that you had to in order to hang out with her is problematic. You can't possibly know all that you want to be or do right this minute, but you probably know what feels right and what feels wrong. Think about the different situations you just wrote about. Below, write what you know felt right and what you know felt wrong.

What felt right? _____

_____

_____

_____

What felt wrong? _____

_____

_____

_____

When you truly belong, you feel comfortable and safe; you are accepted for *who* you are, not *what* you are. Think about your life right now.

Where do you fit in?

_____

_____

_____

Where do you belong?

_____

_____

_____

12 when comparisons hurt

for you to know

Part of building a healthy body image is learning to stop comparing yourself to others. Comparing your body to others is not going to physically change your body and won't help you create healthy space for positive, authentic feelings of self-worth.

One of two things happen when you compare yourself to others:

1. You feel worse about yourself.

   She is eating way less than I am.

   I hate being in pictures with my sister; she is so much prettier than me, and everyone knows it.

2. You judge others and feel better about yourself.

   I can't go anywhere without noticing all the people around me. I hate to admit it, but when I feel like I am the prettiest girl in the room, my confidence goes way up.

   I'm glad I don't look like her.

The characteristics of other people do not take away from, or add to, your own physical attributes. Allowing your body image to be controlled by what other people look like is self-sabotaging.

for you to explore

Using the list below, circle the people you compare yourself to who make you feel worse about yourself.

Random Friends	Peers	Strangers
Family Members	Celebrities	Everyone
Professional Athletes	Close Friends	Other: _____

Now, write down the specific comparisons you make most often.

For example:

My sister is thinner than me.

My best friend is prettier than me.

Your turn: _____

_____

_____

_____

In reality, everyone is unique, and your comparisons might have truth to them. When you add the "than me" at the end of your comparisons, however, they become unhealthy.

Next, rewrite the comparisons you just listed. Keep the label, but take away the comparison.

For example:

My sister is thin.

My best friend is pretty.

Your turn: _____

_____

_____

_____

_____

The next time you find yourself trapped in comparisons that make you feel worse about yourself, try to see those people for what they are, not for what you're not.

explore more

Think about the times you compare yourself to other people and it gives you an ego boost.

What do you get out of the comparison in the short term (a minute, an hour, a day)?

_____

_____

What do you get out of the comparison in the long run (a week, a month, a year)?

_____

_____

What are some thoughts you can substitute your comparisons with?

_____

_____

13 conquer self-doubt

for you to know

Self-doubt is that negative voice inside of your head that makes you second-guess your decisions. When self-doubt takes over, it can greatly influence your body image and hold you back from doing things you enjoy.

Why did I wear that outfit? I looked stupid.

I know everyone was talking about me after I left the party.

I don't know what I should order for lunch. Everyone will probably think I'm a fat loser if I don't order a salad.

My voice sounds like a high-pitched mouse. There is no way I can ever give that speech.

That voice inside your head, the one that tells you that you can't possibly make the right choice, the one that whispers you can't do anything right, is completely wrong. Challenging your self-doubt can help you overcome it.

for you to explore

Let's explore self-doubt by taking a closer look at some of the decisions you are currently facing. Think of at least three things you'd like to do, but that your self-doubt is interfering with your plans for. First, write what it is you want to do. Then, write the worst possible thing that could happen as a result of trying it. Next, write the best possible thing that could happen.

Finally, explore your thoughts and ask yourself, *Am I willing to take the risk?* Ultimately, it's all up to you.

For example:

What I want to do: *Go swimming with my friends and not wear my T-shirt.*

Worst possible scenario: *I'll worry the entire time about my size, and I won't have any fun. Someone might say something rude since I always swim with my shirt on. Everyone will stare at me.*

Best possible scenario: *I'll actually have fun, nobody will even notice, and I won't have a weird tan line.*

Am I willing to take the risk? *Maybe—I'll think about it.*

Your turn:

What I want to do: _____

_____

Worst possible scenario: _____

_____

Best possible scenario: _____

_____

Am I willing to take the risk? _____

_____

What I want to do: _____

_____

Worst possible scenario: _____

_____

Best possible scenario: _____

_____

Am I willing to take the risk? _____

_____

What I want to do: _____

_____

Worst possible scenario: _____

_____

Best possible scenario: _____

_____

Am I willing to take the risk? _____

_____

explore more

Next time something positive happens after you've doubted yourself, take a moment to celebrate it. Use the space below to write about times this happened in the past. Write what your self-doubt was and what actually happened when you took a risk. If you take the time to reinforce the positive outcomes, you are more likely to conquer future self-doubt.

For example:

Self-doubt: *I wanted to color my hair for a long time. When I finally did, it was dramatically different. I was worried that everyone would talk about me.*

What actually happened? *Everyone complimented me and said they loved it. Even strangers told me they liked it.*

How I felt after I took a risk: *Happy and super confident!*

Your turn:

Self-doubt: _____

_____

What actually happened? _____

_____

How I felt after I took a risk: _____

_____

Self-doubt: _____

_____

What actually happened? _____

_____

How I felt after I took a risk: _____

_____

Self-doubt: _____

_____

What actually happened? _____

_____

How I felt after I took a risk: _____

_____

14 slow down

for you to know

Have you ever heard the saying "Stop and smell the roses"? It actually isn't really about smelling or roses; it's about taking the time to slow down and appreciate the beauty around you. It's about being mindful and simply noticing what's been there all along.

As you grow older, it becomes easy to turn your focus inward instead of taking the time to notice the beauty of some of the simplest things in life.

When I was little, I remember collecting things: rocks, shells, clovers, leaves, flowers, anything I found that struck me as beautiful. I'd closely examine each item before I brought it home. I looked for patterns, traced them with my fingers, and held onto them very tightly. I wasn't thinking about the size of my stomach and I never worried about what other people thought. I didn't have to be perfect. I was just me.

—Jessie

Stopping to smell the roses can be a gentle reminder to look for the beauty in things that don't have anything to do with how you look or what obstacles you're dealing with that very second. It helps you to be present and live in the moment, even if it's just for that moment.

for you to explore

For just one day, stop and smell the roses. Look for the things in life that you normally don't pay attention to. Get in touch with your senses: What do you see, hear, feel, smell, and even taste? Write down everything that you notice. Maybe it's the sound of the tiny waterfalls in the creek behind your house. Maybe it's the way the flowers first bloom in the spring or the colors of the leaves in the fall. Or, perhaps you take the time you think you don't have to go to the park or a trail or the river or a stairwell and just sit with yourself to take some long, deep breaths.

Write down everything you notice.

_____

_____

_____

_____

_____

List three unique things that you discovered.

1. _____

2. _____

3. _____

List three things you learned about yourself.

1. _____

2. _____

3. _____

Think about the things you just listed, and let them be a reminder to become more mindful of the world around you. Give yourself permission to live in the moment and enjoy the journey.

explore more

Think back to when you were little. What did you love? What beauty did you see in the things around you that you have stopped noticing?

I used to love playing in the woods behind my house. My friends and I would climb trees, collect rocks and throw them in the creek, and just talk until it got dark and we had to go inside for dinner. I never cared about getting dirty or the bugs or anything else in the world.

—*Sarah*

Use the space below to write your favorite mindful memories from your childhood. Be specific. If you'd like, find something that reminds you of this memory and keep it in a special place to remind you to stay present.

_____

_____

_____

_____

15 you are not alone

for you to know

Sometimes being a girl can feel incredibly lonely. All your feelings and body image blues seem like they are only yours, like you are the only one who feels this way. These feelings are often intense and isolating and difficult to express, but the truth is this: no matter how terrible you feel, you are not alone.

I was at a friend's house, and some other girls came over. At first, I was a little intimidated because I didn't know them very well and one of the girls is really popular. Like, really popular. Like everyone-is-in-love-with-her popular. Everything about her is perfect: perfect family, perfect car, perfect body, perfect skin, perfect hair. Perfect. We were all just sitting around, and someone started talking about weight. Then we all started talking about the different things we hated about our bodies. Even her. I mean, even this girl who has it all wants to look different. I didn't think about it when I was there, but later I realized that we are all going through the same stuff, we just don't talk about it like that. It really helped me to know that I'm not alone.

—Chelsea

A lot of girls struggle with their body image, but not everyone talks about the true intensity of it. Finding evidence that you are not alone is helpful. It can help you find caring people who understand, it can help you reach out for support when you're struggling, and it can provide you with peace of mind simply knowing that you're not alone.

for you to explore

Think about a time when you had a situation similar to the one Chelsea had: a light-bulb moment when you were struggling with your body image, and you came across evidence that someone else was struggling too. It might have been a face-to-face conversation; something over text, e-mail, or social media; something you overheard; or even something you read about or saw on TV.

Describe the situation. _____

_____

How did you feel before the situation? _____

_____

How did you feel during the situation? _____

_____

How did you feel after the situation? _____

_____

What were your thoughts after the situation? _____

_____

How did it change or influence your body image? _____

_____

explore more

Find more evidence that you are not alone with your body image struggles. It may be a conversation you just had with your best friend. You may have overheard strangers talking about their bodies at a coffee shop or read a really powerful poem. Or, you may have found out the girl you thought was perfect really isn't perfect at all because she told you. You are so not alone. List your evidence below.

I know I'm not alone because: _____

_____

I know I'm not alone because: _____

_____

I know I'm not alone because: _____

_____

I know I'm not alone because: _____

_____

I know I'm not alone because: _____

_____

I know I'm not alone because: _____

_____

I know I'm not alone because: _____

_____

I know I'm not alone because: _____

_____

I know I'm not alone because: _____

_____

I know I'm not alone because: _____

_____

16 looking back

for you to know

A lot of twists and turns and unknowns will come up as you navigate through your teenage years. All this turmoil can create quite the body image uproar. The good news is that you can change your mind-set and make even the worst times manageable.

Chances are, you've moved past many moments in your life that have caused a lot of havoc. When you're in these moments, it probably feels like you'll never get out. You may feel like your face won't ever clear up, as though your clothes will never fit right, or you'll never fit in. Most of these moments pass. Congratulations on making it through another section. Wrap this one up by proving to yourself that, indeed, things do get better.

for you to explore

Reflect upon the work you just did, and write five things that you know now but wish you had known earlier.

For example: *I wish I had known that so many other girls feel the same way about their body as I do.*

Your turn:

1. _____

2. _____

3. _____

4. _____

5. _____

explore more

The last seven activities focused on walking down memory lane and making sense out of what it means to be a girl these days. Using the space below, think about which period of time was the hardest for you, and write a letter of encouragement to yourself during that time. Maybe it was a hard week, or maybe it was an entirely terrible summer. Think about what you needed to hear during that time. Remember that, as you grow older, you will have new experiences, new ups and downs and lefts and rights—give yourself permission to grow as a result of these experiences. You deserve that.

Dear Self:

_____

_____

_____

_____

_____

_____

_____

_____

Sincerely,

Part 3
Shattering Societal Standards
(Activities 17–24)

17 real beauty

for you to know

With a few quick clicks, anyone can manipulate a photo on a computer. With programs like Photoshop, it is easy to turn an image into whatever you'd like. Most of the models you see in magazines, movies, and newspapers and on TV and the Internet have been significantly altered—they don't look anything like that in real life.

Wouldn't it be great if each manipulated photo read "Warning: This image isn't real!" under the perfectly altered models? Unfortunately, altered images don't come with a warning label.

> When I look at magazines, I know the models don't really look like that in real life, but it feels impossible to not compare myself to them. Everything looks amazing on them and horrible on me. I think to myself, if I just lost a few pounds or if my shoulders weren't so awkwardly broad, my life would be amazing. I would finally be happy.
>
> —Jada

When models are nipped, tucked, and Photoshopped, it creates an unattainable standard—an image of beauty that is impossible to live up to. Here's the crazy thing: most of the people you look at in magazines don't even exist. It isn't uncommon for photo editors to take the legs off of one woman and paste them onto the body of another. They easily lighten or darken skin, zap away zits, tuck in waists, and lengthen legs. They can flatten stomachs, smooth bumps, and make brown eyes blue. They make butts smaller, breasts bigger, and everything in between. It's no wonder we have so many people unhappy with the way their bodies look. Magazines are not the only offenders—it's all types of media. Becoming more mindful of the media you consume will help you understand that the images you see in all forms of media are not real. *You* are real.

for you to explore

Flip through a fashion magazine and take a mental inventory of the models. Below, briefly summarize how the magazine you chose portrays "the perfect girl." Describe her. What does she look like? What is she wearing? Describe her hair, skin, race, height, weight, eye color, fashion style, and so on.

_____

_____

_____

Now, pick a spot where there are a lot of people. It may be a park by your house, the grocery store, a mall, or a coffee shop; anywhere will work. Then go there and just watch. Notice the real people around you. Don't compare yourself to them; don't judge them. This isn't about comparison or passing judgment; it's about seeing the diversity and reality of the world we live in. Notice what people are wearing, what they are doing, and whom they are with. Notice the body diversity; notice the beauty in the body diversity. Write down what you notice.

_____

_____

_____

_____

_____

What is the difference between what you saw in the magazine and what you saw in real life?

_____

_____

_____

_____

What are some ways that you will continue to notice what is real, instead of what fashion magazines portray as real? For example, will you make an effort not to compare your body to those you see in magazines? Or will you notice the beauty in all shapes and sizes?

_____

_____

_____

_____

_____

_____

explore more

Based on your observations, write your own definition of beauty. What is real beauty?

For example:

Real beauty is *when I take a walk in the woods by my house when it's just started to snow.*

Real beauty is *when all my friends are together and we can't stop laughing.*

Your turn:

Real beauty is: _____

_____

_____

_____

_____

_____

18 you are more than a number

for you to know

The society we live in makes it almost impossible to not be influenced by numbers in regard to size, weight, food, and exercise. The media is masterful at making us obsess about these numbers. These numbers have nothing to do with who you are as a person. You are more than a number.

Think about all the numbers our society obsesses over: weight, body mass index (BMI), age, height, bra size, jean size, dress size, carb grams, fat grams, calories, how many times a week you "should" work out, and so on. It doesn't end, does it? It's easy to get caught up in what you "should" be worried about, which can create patterns of faulty thinking. Faulty thinking is when your thoughts about yourself are inaccurate and you draw conclusions without any real proof or evidence.

For example:

I just ate like a million grams of fat. I'm so gross.

All the other girls wear super-skinny jeans, and they probably don't even make my size in them.

I have to work out every day this week or else I'll be huge.

These thoughts are fueled by society's unhealthy standards and are examples of how faulty thinking can get in your way. These numbers do not define you. *You* get to define you. You can begin to do this by changing your faulty thoughts to realistic thoughts. Realistic thoughts are when you look at the reality of a situation (the positive, the negative, and everything in between) before jumping to a conclusion. Realistic thoughts are balanced and based on facts and evidence.

for you to explore

The societal emphasis on numbers isn't likely to change. You can't control that. What you can control is how you react to these numbers and how you allow them to affect your life. Below, reread each girl's faulty thought and write an example of a more realistic thought.

For example:

Faulty thought: *I just ate like a million grams of fat. I'm so gross.*

Realistic thought: *Fat grams don't make you gross. And I probably didn't eat a million.*

Your turn:

Faulty thought: *All the other girls wear super-skinny jeans, and they probably don't even make them in my size.*

Realistic thought: _____

_____

Faulty thought: *I have to work out every day this week or else I'll be huge.*

Realistic thought: _____

_____

Now, list a few examples of your own faulty thoughts that are number driven, and combat them with realistic thinking.

Faulty thought: _____

_____

Realistic thought: _____

_____

Faulty thought: _____

_____

Realistic thought: _____

_____

Faulty thought: _____

_____

Realistic thought: _____

_____

explore more

Below, list all the numbers you have used to define yourself. They might be some of the same things you just wrote about, or they may be related to other things, like the number of times you struck out in a softball game, your GPA, or your SAT score.

_____

_____

_____

_____

_____

_____

_____

_____

Now, using your list, write *I'm more than* in front of what you just listed. For example: *I'm more than the size of my jeans.* If you feel yourself obsessing about numbers again, look back at this page to remind yourself that you're so much more than a number.

19 false advertising

for you to know

An advertisement is never just an advertisement. When it comes to most ads targeting teen girls, the message that is being sent is this: "There is something wrong with you or your body, and our product is going to fix it."

How many times have you read a magazine, only to feel like you immediately have to go shopping? That is the point of advertising; they want you to buy the product they are selling. The problem is most of the time the products that promise a quick fix generally don't work. Think about the last time you bought a new product and couldn't wait to use it, only to be disappointed by the results.

I keep breaking out and always buy everything I see advertised to clear up my skin. I have an entire drawer full of acne products that didn't help. Nothing ever works, even though I am always hopeful that it will.

—Camilla

My best friend started taking some diet pills she saw advertised in a fitness magazine. One day, she started shaking and got really dizzy. Her mom took her to the doctor, and her heart rate was way too high, and her blood pressure was way too low. The ad promised the pills would make her feel healthier, but she only took a few, and they could have actually killed her. It was so scary.

—Marla

I saved up to buy this really expensive shampoo because my curly hair is always out of control. I literally thought my life was going to change and couldn't wait to use it. All it did was make my hair super greasy and flat. And guess what? A few hours later it was all frizzy again.

—Charley

It's perfectly fine (and fun) to go shopping and try out new things. But most products don't deliver what they promise and can easily leave you feeling badly about yourself and your body. The next activity is about building awareness and being mindful of the media's goals. With practice and knowledge, you can teach yourself to not get sucked into the hype.

for you to explore

Think about a time you bought a product that you "had to have"—something you saw advertised and convinced yourself that you needed—that didn't work at all.

What was the product? _____

_____

What did you think it would do? _____

_____

What did it actually do? _____

_____

Now, rewrite the advertisement to reflect the truth. Be sassy.

For example:

A mascara ad reads: "Double the length of your lashes."

Ad truth: "Double the length? Try giant black clumps that take forever to wash out."

Your turn:

Ad reads: _____

_____

Ad truth: _____

_____

Now, think of a few more examples of advertisements that didn't do what they promised.

Ad reads: _____

_____

Ad truth: _____

_____

Ad reads: _____

_____

Ad truth: _____

_____

Ad reads: _____

_____

Ad truth: _____

_____

explore more

Find a fashion magazine, and read through it. Fold down each page that contains an advertisement that promises to change how you look. *"Touchable smooth locks."* Fold down pages with contradictions, like an article about positive self-esteem with an advertisement for makeup on the same page. Fold down pages with gimmicks or lies. *"Reduce redness and pimple size in just four hours."* Fold down pages that have completely unhealthy messages. *"Lose ten pounds in ten days."* You can also fold down all the pages with ads that seem completely insane, like a woman washing a car in really high heels and short shorts, all sudsy and sexy. Think about the falsehoods behind these kinds of messages. Really, how many women do you know who wash cars in high heels? Sometimes it's hard to see what is right in front of you unless you are really looking. Once you've finished folding down the pages, look at what is left.

What do you notice? What is left to read? _____

_____

How do you typically feel after reading a fashion magazine? _____

_____

How does this change the way you will look at a fashion magazine the next time you read one?

_____

_____

for you to know

Fat talk, simply stated, is when people have negative conversations about the size and shape of their bodies. Females are notorious for engaging in fat talk. Engaging in fat talk reinforces the ridiculous societal standard that you have to be dissatisfied with your body. Fat talk is completely unhealthy and keeps women and girls at war with their bodies.

Speaking negatively about our bodies has become so normalized in our society that you might not even realize when you or someone else is doing it. People engage in fat talk for a variety of reasons: for connection, for validation, to judge others, and to not seem overly confident about themselves.

"Does my butt look big in these pants?"

"I can't believe she just ate all of that!"

"I have, like, zero muscle tone."

"You look super cute in that outfit—have you lost weight?"

"I wish I had her body."

"I'd have a date to homecoming if I wasn't so fat."

"I have wiggly grandma arms."

"Hello, cellulite."

"She shouldn't wear that."

"I ate way too much. I shouldn't have ordered dessert."

"I need a boob job."

"I look like a stuffed sausage in this shirt."

This list could go on for pages. Some of the statements listed above may seem positive, but if you look closely, you'll see that they still reinforce the idea that thin equals better. For example, "You look super cute in that outfit—have you lost weight?" may seem positive, but what message does it really send? "You looked terrible before, but now you look fabulous!" That's not a compliment; it's a backhanded put-down. When you think about it, what does fat talk really accomplish?

Maggy: "I ate way too much. I shouldn't have ordered dessert."

Kelsey: "OMG, look at what I ate! It was way more than you, and my dessert is twice the size of yours!"

For the record, they both will probably eat their desserts. This particular fat-talk conversation is serving as validation for each girl to feel OK about eating dessert. Fat talk typically *does not* go like this:

Maggy: "I have wiggly grandma arms."

Kelsey: "Yeah, you kind of do. You should work on that."

That is a really mean comment and definitely not the validation that Maggy was probably looking for. Fat talk is a societal problem, but it doesn't have to be your problem. With practice, you can end fat talk and also encourage those who are close to you to do the same.

for you to explore

When you make a negative remark about your body to another person, how are you really feeling? What do you really need to hear? What is your goal? Think about the last few times you have used fat talk to convey a feeling, and complete the questions below.

For example:

When I said, *"I look like a cow in every pair of pants I own"* to *my friend Renee*, I was feeling *self-conscious*. What I really needed was *to connect with someone*. Next time, instead of fat talking, I can accomplish this by *reaching out to a friend I trust and know I can be myself around.*

Your turn:

When I said, _____ to

_____, I was feeling _____. What I really needed

was _____. Next time, instead of

fat talking, I can accomplish this by _____.

When I said, _____ to

_____, I was feeling _____. What I really needed

was _____. Next time, instead of

fat talking, I can accomplish this by _____.

activity 20 ✳ replace fat talk

When I said, _____ to

_____, I was feeling _____. What I really needed

was _____. Next time, instead of

fat talking, I can accomplish this by _____.

explore more

Fat talk is toxic and unnecessary, but also a hard habit to break if you do it often. Let's try to break this habit, once and for all. Get a blank piece of paper and something to write with. If you'd like, use color. In the middle of the paper, write *No More Fat Talk*. Now, use the rest of the space surrounding those words to write down all the fat-talk phrases that you have said in the past. When you are finished, pledge to yourself to eliminate fat talk from your daily interactions and conversations. Rip up your paper. If you catch yourself in a fat-talk conversation, remember this exercise. Eliminating fat talk might take time and practice, but it will be worth it. You have much better things to talk about.

21 face fat talk

for you to know

You just learned how to replace fat talk; now it is time to face fat talk. Chances are high that you will come in contact with someone in the near future who makes a negative remark about her body. You have the tools to change the conversation and turn fat talk around.

When you first decide to take a stand against fat talk, you may face a bit of adversity. Some people are so used to using fat talk as a conversation tool that they don't see anything wrong with it.

I first learned about fat talk at school. It was Love Your Body Day, and we watched a cool video and talked about it in class. Until then, I never realized how much I did it. It was all my friends and I talked about and was totally unhealthy. I started to notice how almost every female around me put her body down—even my mom and my swim coach! Now, each time they do it, I either call them out or change the subject. It's really empowering, and I feel better about myself.

—Stella

Just like Stella, you have the power to choose what you do and don't put up with. Fat talk is deeply engrained in people, and as you are now aware, it takes practice to reduce it. You can help yourself and those you care about by facing the conversation. When you hear someone else fat talking, you have a few options for addressing it.

Option 1: Confront. This is tricky, but doable. When someone uses fat talk around you, speak up. Confront her and tell her what you know about fat talk and how unhealthy it is. You might say something like: "It makes me sad when you talk badly about your body, because I think you're beautiful." Confronting is easier when you know the person really well, like with a close friend or family member. Share your feelings and politely ask her to stop.

Option 2: Don't participate in the conversation. There will be times when no matter what you say, you are not going to make other people stop using fat talk. For example, adults who have been dieting on and off their whole lives are very slow to change. It's also that "realm of control" thing we discussed in the last section. You cannot control what they say or do, but you can choose not to engage in the conversation. Sometimes actions speak way louder than words.

Option 3: Change the subject. Depending on the person, changing the subject might be the best option. This way, you are not participating in the conversation, and you're cutting it off.

Remember, you don't have to put up with fat talk. You have the power to challenge societal standards by choosing what you do, and don't, allow into your life.

for you to explore

Using the three tips listed above, practice what you might say the next time you are confronted with fat talk.

For example:

Your best friend says to you: "OMG, do I look like a beached whale in this dress? Be honest! I don't know why I'm even wearing it."

Option 1: Confront. *"Have you ever heard about fat talk? A lot of girls put their bodies down and have completely unhealthy conversations with each other about their sizes. For the record, you look great, but I think it's so sad how we always do this. I'd like to make a pact with you that we will both stop bashing our bodies. We have better things to talk about. Deal?"*

Option 2: Don't participate in the conversation. *"I'm not even going to answer that,"* or you could completely ignore the comment.

Option 3: Change the subject. *"So, did you study for the psych test we have next week?"* There is a chance, with this particular scenario, that if you decided to not participate in the conversation, or changed the subject, the girl would say, "I knew I looked disgusting" or something of the sort. If this happens, you'd have to confront her: "No, I don't think you look disgusting, but I chose not to answer you because I really don't like it when you put your body down."

Your turn:

You and a friend from school decide to go bathing-suit shopping for an upcoming pool party. The entire time your friend makes comments about how terrible she looks, how she is going to be the biggest one there, and how she needs a boob job. What could you do?

Confront: _____

_____

_____

_____

Don't participate in the conversation: _____

_____

_____

Change the subject: _____

_____

_____

_____

explore more

Comebacks are a great way to stop a behavior. Being prepared for a comeback will give you the courage to say what you are truly feeling. Below, list the top three fat-talk phrases that you hear most often from your friends or family.

1. _____

2. _____

3. _____

Now, list what you just wrote in the space provided below and think of some clever comebacks you can use to combine all three of the tips you just practiced.

For example:

Fat talk: *"Ughhh, I feel so fat."*

Comeback: *"It's normal to have days when you don't feel so great about your body. I've noticed that we spend a lot of time saying negative things about ourselves; let's not do that anymore. I'm trying to have a better attitude about myself."*

Your turn:

Fat talk: _____

Comeback: _____

_____

_____

Fat talk: _____

Comeback: _____

_____

_____

Fat talk: _____

Comeback: _____

_____

_____

22 break up with your scale

for you to know

Have you ever woken up feeling fabulous until you stepped on the scale, and all of a sudden it felt like the worst day ever? Why do so many females let the number on the scale determine if they are going to have an awesome or terrible day? The scale can only tell you what you weigh. It cannot measure your talent, intelligence, wisdom, strength, or anything else.

Our society gives the scale entirely too much power. Here's the truth: The number on the scale is just a number. It isn't a reflection of who you are on the inside. Plus, small shifts in weight are completely normal and to be expected during your teen years.

The first thing I do every morning is weigh myself. I can wake up in an awesome mood, and even if I weigh .05 pounds more than I did the day before, then goodbye awesome mood. If it's more than that, I feel gross and wear sweatpants to school.

—Marissa

OMG, my mother is a slave to the scale. She weighs herself all the time. Once, I saw her weigh herself, sigh, take off her bracelet, and weigh herself again! I asked her if she really thought her bracelet would make her weigh less, and she rolled her eyes at me and said "One day you'll understand." I hope I never understand that!

—Jennifer

I'm overweight and am working with a dietitian to eat healthier and lose weight safely. The problem is the scale. Sometimes it totally derails me. I'll make healthy choices, work out, and feel great, but some weeks the number doesn't budge. Then I feel like I'm not making any progress, and I feel like giving up. It's totally psychological because I feel better and healthier. I wish scales had never been invented.

—Ashley

Think about this: If you have a small shift in your weight and didn't have the scale to tell you, would you even notice? Breaking ties with your scale can help you gain a healthier sense of self based on who you are on the *inside*, which is more important.

for you to explore

The first step in letting go of your scale is deciding you are going to do it. The next step is recognizing how much the number influences your feelings. To help get yourself started, answer the following questions:

How do you feel if the number on the scale is where you want it to be?

_____

How do you feel if the number on the scale isn't where you want it to be?

_____

What are the things you tell yourself if the number on the scale is where you want it to be?

_____

_____

What are the things you tell yourself if the number on the scale isn't where you want it to be?

_____

_____

What do you notice about your responses to those questions?

_____

_____

Now, using your responses as a guide, write a breakup letter to your scale. Write your letter as if you were ending a serious long-term relationship, because essentially, that is what you are doing. When you are finished, read your letter over and over and over again. Remember: you are not a number.

Dear Scale:

_____

_____

_____

_____

_____

_____

_____

_____

_____

Sincerely,

explore more

Now that you've broken up with your scale, bash it or banish it. You can donate it, throw it away, or literally bash it. Note: if the scale does not belong to you, ask the person who owns it to hide it or keep it out of sight, or talk to that person about this activity and ask permission to bash it. You'll need a hammer or a baseball bat and a giant plastic bag. Put the scale in the bag and tie it tightly (there will likely be pieces of plastic flying around that you don't want in your eyes). When the bag is securely tied, bash it. Enjoy the process of breaking up with yet another number game.

23 stop apologizing for how you look

for you to know

It is one thing to apologize when you have done something that warrants a genuine apology, like spilling your best friend's deepest secret or breaking a promise. But apologizing for how you look is never necessary.

Our society earns a gold medal in tearing women down because of how they look. Glance at any magazine cover in the grocery store, and you are likely to read a headline that puts down a woman because she (a) appears to have gained weight, (b) left the house without makeup on, (c) wore something that somebody didn't like, or (d) has a different hairstyle. In fact, it is highly likely that you will find a few magazines with all of the above on one single cover! This is a perfect example of how girls are conditioned to apologize for how they look.

> *I apologize for everything. If I walk up to friends and one of them is more dressed up than me, I apologize. If my lips are chapped, I apologize. If I went to the gym and didn't have time to shower, I tell everyone I didn't shower and apologize for it. I apologize if my legs are dry and ashy and I need lotion, if my clothes are wrinkled, or if I think my clothes are too tight. I'm always saying sorry for how I look. I'm not really sorry—I just say it.*
>
> *—Jillian*

Apologizing for how you look serves as protection from other people's criticism but can make you seem insecure. The need to apologize for how you look is completely internal, unhelpful, and unnecessary. It's not always about body image, either. Spend a moment thinking about other things you apologize for that you're not really sorry for. Over-apologizing is something that girls and women are taught to do. You don't have to apologize for things you are not genuinely sorry for. With practice and awareness, you can attack the unhelpful thoughts and learn to stop pointlessly apologizing.

for you to explore

You can learn how to stop apologizing for how you look. First, write down the last time you did this.

Whom did you apologize to? _____

_____

What did you apologize for? _____

_____

Now, dig deeper into your need to apologize for how you look. Use your responses above to answer the following questions:

What evidence did you have that you actually needed to apologize? _____

_____

How do you react when a friend apologizes for how she looks? _____

_____

When you apologize for how you look, what are you most worried about?

_____

_____

How do you feel after you apologize for how you look? Really, does it make you feel better? A lot better?

_____

_____

How do you think you would feel if you didn't apologize for how you look?

_____

_____

What would be the worst thing that could happen if you never apologized for how you look again?

_____

_____

What are the positive things you would gain if you could just be yourself?

_____

_____

_____

_____

explore more

You have the right to be you without apologizing for it. Just being yourself might mean sometimes you don't have time to take a shower, sometimes your hair is messy, sometimes you are over- or underdressed, and sometimes your skin isn't covered in makeup. It's not a big deal. Below, list the top five things you apologize for and then write ...no big deal.

For example:

I left the house without makeup on today...no big deal.

I am completely period bloated...no big deal.

Your turn:

1. _____

2. _____

3. _____

4. _____

5. _____

Starting right now, let your no-big-deal list serve as a constant reminder that it is OK to just be you.

24 shatter societal standards

for you to know

Our society is powerful. The media we consume are filled with hidden messages and innuendos that are highly influential and can negatively impact how you think and feel about yourself and your body.

Hopefully this section has taught you a few defense mechanisms and coping skills to handle all the crazy reality of living in today's society. We live in a world that is fixated on beauty and looks and sizes and shapes. The media provides us with a steady flow of messages that indirectly whisper, "You're not good enough." The unfortunate part is that it isn't easy to escape these messages. But now you are armed with the truth: you are good enough, and you don't need anyone else to tell you that. Photos are digitally altered to appear flawless. You're not a size, shape, or number. Advertisers want you to feel badly about your body and looks so that you buy their products. Fat talk is pointless; you have way more important things to talk about. The number on the scale is just a number, and that number doesn't have the power to define you—at all. The scale is just a machine. And you don't ever need to apologize for being you. Ever.

for you to explore

List five of society's unhealthy standards that have negatively impacted you the most. Then, using what you've learned, write a new, healthy standard.

For example:

Unhealthy standard: *I should have a perfect model body.*

My healthy standard: *Models are not perfect, and I don't have to look like them.*

Your turn:

Unhealthy standard: _____

My healthy standard: _____

Unhealthy standard: _____

My healthy standard: _____

Unhealthy standard: _____

My healthy standard: _____

Unhealthy standard: _____

My healthy standard: _____

Unhealthy standard: _____

My healthy standard: _____

explore more

The last seven activities focused on shattering the unhealthy standards that society places on young women. Using the space below, freewrite about what surprised you the most in these activities and how you'll act differently as a result.

_____

_____

_____

_____

_____

_____

_____

_____

Part 4
Use Your Voice
(Activities 25–32)

25 find your voice

for you to know

You can probably recall a situation where you wanted to speak up, but didn't. Afterward, you may have ruminated about what you wanted to say for hours, days, or even weeks—wishing you would have just said what was on your mind.

Most people have been in a situation where they wanted to speak up, but for one reason or another, they didn't.

My friends and I went to dinner a few weekends ago, and I was having a great time until they started saying really mean things about a girl who was sitting near us. They made fun of her hair, her weight, what she was eating, and what she was wearing. I tried to change the subject, but it didn't work. I really wanted to tell my friends to stop, but I was afraid they would think I was lame. I got really quiet, and everyone kept asking me what was wrong. I said, "Nothing." I wanted to say they were being rude and also that it made me uncomfortable. It's been two weeks, and I'm still really mad at myself for not speaking up and really mad at them for being so mean.

—Laila

I go over conversations I have had with people in my head so many times it makes me crazy. I pick apart what I "should" have said, but never have the courage to actually say it. I'm always afraid I'll sound stupid, someone will think I am overreacting, or someone will make fun of me.

—Kelly

I never speak up. I don't know why. Even over stupid things, like when my friends ask me where I want to go for lunch, I say, "I don't care," and we end up going somewhere I don't like. Then I get mad. Everyone says I'm the quiet one, but my head is never quiet.

—Anya

Speaking up isn't easy. It's especially difficult when what you have to say might not be popular or there is a possibility you may be rejected. Each person's experience with speaking up is going to be different. Finding your voice and gathering the courage to actually use it can improve your self-confidence tremendously and improve your overall self-image.

for you to explore

Complete the following statements:

A time I wanted to speak up but didn't was: _____

_____

I chose not to speak up because: _____

_____

_____

What I wanted to say was: _____

_____

_____

What I actually said was: _____

_____

_____

If I were faced with the same situation today, I would say: _____

_____

_____

explore more

Have you ever heard of the term "thought bubble"? It's a cartoon drawing that looks like a cloud and represents someone's thoughts. In the thought bubble below, list some things that you would like to say to someone else, but haven't. For example: *I need your help. I'm sorry I said that. I don't like it when you talk to me like that. I am glad we're friends. I've been working here for three summers and think I deserve a raise.* When you're done writing down your thoughts, practice saying a few of them out loud. Just practice. You can practice in the mirror or on a walk by yourself, or even talk to a trusted friend or adult. Notice all the things you need to say and reflect upon what it would feel like to actually say them to the person.

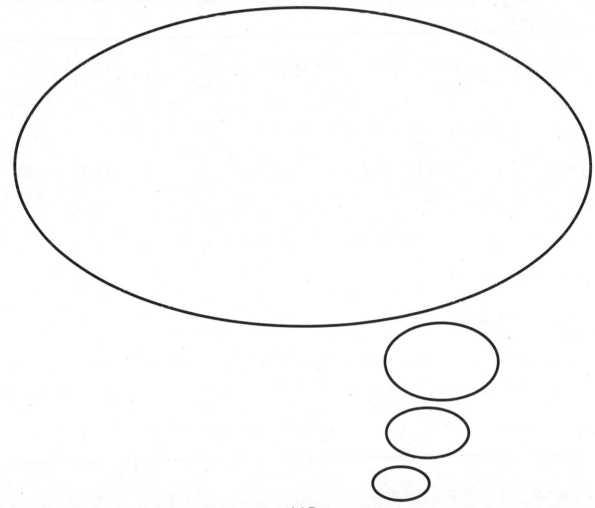

26 learn to take a compliment

for you to know

Many girls don't know how to accept a sincere kudo. In fact, many girls easily turn a genuine compliment into a body-bashing session without even realizing it. With practice, you can learn to take a compliment with ease. Perhaps you may even enjoy the moment.

Has anyone ever given you a compliment, only for you to immediately discount every word she said? Or you felt the need to reject the praise by immediately complimenting the person back? Taking a compliment can be hard, especially if you don't believe what the other person is saying.

Abbey: "I love your outfit! You're so stylish!"

Emily: "Really? I look like a cow. I tried on a hundred things this morning, and everything looked awful. But you look super cute, as always."

Abbey: "Ugh. I couldn't find anything clean. I probably smell—nobody wants to be near me today."

Emily: "You're crazy. I'm always way grosser than you."

Or how about this:

Dani: "Great job on your presentation today!"

Maria: "You did so much better; everyone did. I sounded like an idiot and was sweating, and my face got all splotchy."

Dani: "Seriously? You were awesome. I sucked and probably failed."

Accepting a compliment might be difficult for many reasons. You may not believe you deserve the compliment. Or, you may not want to seem like you are bragging by accepting the compliment. Take another look at what Maria did when Dani complimented her presentation; she immediately bashed herself and pointed out things that nobody else would have even noticed. And think about this: when you turn down a compliment, it may insult the person complimenting you. The best way to respond to a compliment is to simply say thank you.

for you to explore

When someone says something nice to you or about you, just say, "Thank you." You don't have to give the other person a compliment in return, which may sound forced and not entirely genuine. Don't put yourself or your body down after receiving a compliment either. Below are a few typical, generic compliments. Using what you now know, write down how you would respond. This is the easiest activity ever; just write, *Thank you.* Moving forward, when someone gives you a compliment, just say, "Thank you." That's it. No explaining, no complimenting back. "Thank you." "Thanks." "Merci." "Gracias." It's so simple, and you can do it!

For example:

Compliment: *Congrats on passing your driving test.*

Response: *Thank you.*

Your turn:

Compliment: *Your hair looks fabulous!*

Response: _____

Compliment: *I heard you got the job—congrats!*

Response: _____

Compliment: *Is that a new dress? I love that color on you!*

Response: _____

Compliment: *You handled that situation well; I would have been furious.*

Response: _____

Compliment: *Great game today!*

Response: _____

explore more

Now that you have practiced *receiving* a compliment, it's time to practice *giving* a compliment. Specifically, it's important to compliment people for things other than their looks. Below, list at least five compliments you can give someone that have nothing to do with what the person looks like. You can list more if you'd like. Challenge yourself to start giving well-deserved compliments that are not appearance-based.

For example:

"Great job on your test; I know you studied hard."

"That was cool of you to invite her to sit with us."

Your turn:

1. _____

2. _____

3. _____

4. _____

5. _____

set healthy boundaries 27

for you to know

Personal boundaries are all about your own thoughts and feelings, and separating your needs from others' needs. Boundaries, like saying no and setting limits, are difficult to set but can be incredibly liberating. When you set a healthy boundary, it means you value yourself—your whole entire self.

"Sugar and spice, and everything nice…" You can probably finish that old saying, right? Girls are taught from a young age to be polite and nice, which often leads to abundantly trying to please everybody. This might mean saying yes when you really mean no or putting up with someone else's bad behavior or negative influence when you really want to tell him or her to stop. Setting a healthy boundary means speaking up for yourself and creating your own personal rules for your friendships and relationships. It can be difficult to set boundaries if you

- believe that you're not worth it

- think it's your job to make other people happy

- are afraid of someone else's reaction of if you say no or set a healthy boundary

- are trying to fit in with a certain group

- feel self-conscious and are really worried about what other people think about you.

Another barrier to setting healthy boundaries is the fear of how someone may react to having the boundary set, especially if they are used to you caving. Someone else might

- minimize your feelings: "you are totally overreacting"

- try to make you feel guilty: "I guess you don't care about me"

- hold your friendship hostage: "Fine, don't go with us. We will never ask you again"

- post photos or make comments on social media to try to make you jealous: "We had the best night ever. Too bad a certain someone wasn't with us."

Despite what other people think or how they react, boundaries are important in every aspect of your life. They keep you focused on what you want, instead of confused by others' expectations of you. Learning to set boundaries often starts with saying no to things you don't want to do.

for you to explore

Listed below are examples of situations where it may be difficult to say no. If you were in the situation, you might feel torn or worry the other person would be mad at you if you said no. Read each situation, and practice saying no. While writing your response, be firm, don't give a million excuses, and stick to your word.

For example:

Situation: Your friend is having a party, and you don't want to go. There are going to be people there you don't care for, and you'd rather just chill at your house. Your friend keeps begging you to go, saying she has to have you with her or the party will not be fun. She says you both can leave early and are just staying for a minute, which you know won't happen.

Say no: "Thanks for the invite, but I am staying in tonight. Maybe next time I'll go."

Your turn:

Situation: Your friends want to make a video of you all being silly and upload it to the Internet. You are up for being silly and having fun, but you don't want it online. Plus, you know your parents will be furious if they find out.

Say no: _____

_____

Situation: All of your friends are going to see a movie that you don't want to see, and they keep begging you to go. You have a ton of homework to do, plus you don't really feel well.

Say no: _____

_____

Situation: Your sister asks to borrow a new shirt of yours that you've never even worn. The last time she borrowed something, she ruined it and promised she would pay you back. That was months ago, and she has never mentioned it again.

Say no: _____

_____

explore more

Respond to the following questions:

Which situation above would be the hardest for you to say no to? Why?

_____

_____

What other situations have you been in where you said yes, when you really meant no?

_____

_____

Whom do you have the most trouble saying no to?

_____

_____

What are the benefits of saying no to something you don't want to do?

_____

_____

28 confidence vs. conceit

for you to know

Girls are often taught (and sometimes told) to not talk about their strengths and accomplishments. When you silence your strengths and your accomplishments, it can lead to body shame. Being proud of your accomplishments is not being conceited; it's being self-confident.

Being confident means that you believe in yourself and your abilities and you are generally proud of your accomplishments. When you are conceited, you have an embellished opinion about yourself or your abilities, and you incessantly brag about them. Conceited people are often really insecure and feel the need to talk about themselves in order to get praise. Being confident about your body, your looks, and your achievements attracts others to you, whereas conceit can turn people away.

Confidence	Conceit
"I look fabulous today!"	*"I look so much better than everyone here."*
"I aced my final!"	*"I got the highest grade in the class; I'm so much smarter than everyone here."*
"My new haircut feels great."	*"My hair is amazing; my stylist told me I have the best hair she's ever worked with."*

See the difference? Many girls are hesitant to share things they are proud of out of the fear that others will think they are acting braggy or conceited. There is a huge difference. Sharing things that are important to you—especially with the people who matter to you—will increase your self-confidence and help others see the real you.

for you to explore

Read each story below and circle whether it's confidence or conceit.

1. Jessica was asked to the prom by a few people but acts as though everyone in the school asked her. She talks about it nonstop even though she knows her best friend hasn't been asked by anyone.

    Confidence   Conceit

2. Lily scored the winning goal in the soccer game last weekend against a really tough team. When her friends asked her how the game went, she told them that she scored the winning goal and was really happy about it.

    Confidence   Conceit

3. Caroline was accepted to all of her top college choices. She texted all her closest friends and invited them to dinner with her family to celebrate.

    Confidence   Conceit

4. Dania constantly talks about how rich her family is, what kind of car she is going to get, and how she is so much prettier than everyone else.

    Confidence   Conceit

1. Conceit
2. Confidence
3. Confidence
4. Conceit

explore more

Honestly answer the following questions:

What are you good at? _____

_____

What are you proud of? _____

_____

What is the top thing you hide from others? _____

_____

What do you want others to know about you? _____

_____

What are some ways you can begin to *tell* others what you are proud of?

_____

_____

What are some ways you can begin to *show* others what you are proud of?

_____

_____

identifying emotional 29
triggers

for you to know

A trigger is the cause of a situation. Similar to when someone pulls the trigger of a gun, an emotional trigger can cause you to implode with feelings. You might be triggered by other people, or things you see, hear, smell, touch, or taste.

When it comes to body image, there are tons of things that can easily trigger you into feeling badly about yourself and your body.

- "I went to a party, and this girl complimented everyone in my group except for me. I felt so badly about my body that I wanted to cry. The rest of the party was total torture."

- "At lunch yesterday, everyone was talking about thigh gaps. They started to compare how much space was in between their thighs. I felt so out of place and then felt terrible about myself. They probably think I'm a whale."

- "Everyone always posts pictures of themselves online, and they all look perfect and like they're having so much fun. I always feel so left out and completely ugly."

Body image triggers are completely individualized, meaning what sets you off or makes you implode might not do the same to someone else. There are many examples of situations that can trigger you, but the good news is that you have control over how you react. Identifying your emotional triggers can help you learn to cope with thoughts, feelings, and behaviors associated with them.

for you to explore

Read each triggering scenario below as if it applied to you, and identify the actual trigger and feeling associated with each situation. Then, write a solution to avoid or cope with the trigger.

For example:

"When I read fashion magazines, I always feel fat and frumpy and like I need new makeup and clothes."

Trigger: *reading fashion magazines*

Feeling: *fat and frumpy*

Solution: *Don't read fashion magazines, or if I do, prepare myself beforehand by saying "Those girls are not real."*

Your turn:

"We live near the beach and hang out by the ocean a lot during the summer. When we invite guys, they always comment on other girls' bodies. It makes me so self-conscious. I never want to walk in front of them."

Trigger: _____

Feeling: _____

Solution: _____

"At every holiday, everyone talks about how pretty and skinny my sister is. I don't wear preppy clothes like she does, and I have short, spiky hair. They think I'm weird, and I always end up feeling invisible and judged."

Trigger: _____

Feeling: _____

Solution: _____

"My best friend is a selfie addict and is always taking pictures to post online. When we are together (which is always), she won't put her phone down. It's so annoying. She is way more connected than me on social media, and everyone comments on how pretty she is, but they never say anything about me. I feel ugly and gross and awful around her and wish she'd stop taking pictures."

Trigger: _____

Feeling: _____

Solution: _____

explore more

Think about some situations when you were feeling great, and then all of a sudden, something triggered you, and you felt terrible. Below, identify your top three triggers (you can list more if you'd like), how you felt before the trigger and after the trigger, and how you can productively cope with the trigger. In the future, when something triggers you, remember how you felt before the triggering situation occurred. You are still that girl.

For example:

Triggering situation: *My mom asked me if I've gained weight.*

How I felt before: *Great. I was headed over to a friend's house to watch a movie.*

How I felt after: *I felt terrible and changed my clothes and was in a bad mood all night. It made me not want to eat anything at my friend's house, and all I thought about was how fat I am.*

Ways I can cope in the future: *I can tell my mom how her comments make me feel and set a healthy boundary with her to not talk about my weight.*

Your turn:

Triggering situation: _____

How I felt before: _____

How I felt after: _____

Ways I can cope in the future: _____

_____

Triggering situation: _____

How I felt before: _____

How I felt after: _____

Ways I can cope in the future: _____

_____

Triggering situation: _____

How I felt before: _____

How I felt after: _____

Ways I can cope in the future: _____

_____

30 "I'm fine"

for you to know

The sentence "I'm fine" can mean so many different things. The reality is "I'm fine" never really means "I'm fine."

When you say, "I'm fine," what do you really mean? "Fine" is a generic term that a lot of girls say merely out of habit. You may ask your friend how her day was and hear her reply with, "It was fine." Perhaps you're feeling overwhelmed and had the worst weekend imaginable and someone asks, "What's wrong?" "Nothing, I'm fine" is your go-to reply. Sometimes, you may, indeed, be OK. Other times, "I'm fine" is code for

- "I don't want to talk about it."

- "You need to guess and ask me a million times what's wrong. I probably still won't tell you, but you need to keep asking."

- "I'm not fine but am going to tell you I am and be ridiculously upset if you don't ask me what is wrong again."

- "I'm sad but don't know how to ask for help."

- "I'm hurt but don't know how to tell you."

- "I'm really pissed at you but am afraid if I tell you that you'll be mad at me and I'll end up apologizing."

- "Don't ask me any more questions."

You can probably think of at least a dozen more coded meanings for the expression. Using the word "fine" keeps you from accurately identifying and naming your emotions. Let's say you are not fine, but you don't want to talk about it (which is OK, as long as you really don't want to talk about it).

Brooklyn: "What's wrong?"

Tess: "I have a lot going on, but don't really want to talk about it…but thanks for asking."

Or, you do want to talk about it:

Brooklyn: "What's wrong?"

Tess: "I have a lot going on right now. Can we chat later? I could really use your advice."

It takes practice, patience, vulnerability, and time to erase the term *fine* from your vocabulary, but in the long run, it's worth it.

for you to explore

What does your "I'm fine" typically mean? Think about all the times someone asked you how you were and you replied, "Fine." Or maybe someone asked you what was wrong and you replied with "Nothing, I'm fine," when you really weren't. Grab something to write with, use color if you'd like, and in the box below, write what your "fine" really means.

"I'm fine" means:

explore more

Challenge yourself to go at least one week without using the word *fine* to describe how you're feeling. Instead, try being honest. Even if you are fine, pick another word to use (refer to the feelings list from the beginning of the book if you are having trouble coming up with one). If you slip, keep trying until you are successful. When you accomplish the one-week goal, work on another week. Keep doing this until you erase the word from your vocabulary and use your voice to let others really know how you're honestly feeling.

31 body language

for you to know

Did you know that we mostly communicate nonverbally? Your body language conveys powerful messages and speaks volumes about how you feel about yourself and your body, without you ever having to say a word.

Your body language is an incredible communication tool. Sometimes people confuse body language with facial expressions. Your body language involves your entire body, from head to toe, whereas your facial expression obviously only involves your face. What makes body language so powerful is that it can change other people's perceptions of you, both positively and negatively, and it can have an impact on how you feel about yourself.

> *I am really uncomfortable with my body, and I know I show it. I wear clothes that are way too big, I don't like to be in front of people, I slouch when I'm sitting, and I act totally standoffish. Sometimes I twirl my hair or mess with my earrings because I am uncomfortable. People always ask me what's wrong and if I'm mad. I don't mean to be rude or always act this way; I'm just so self-conscious.*
>
> *—Katy*

Katy has a clear example here of how body language can impact another person's perceptions. How she feels about her body impacts what other people think about her, and she worries about seeming standoffish. What if Katy wore clothes that fit her better, didn't slouch, and didn't fidget when other people were talking to her? What if she looked more approachable? Do you think she'd attract more people? Your body language has the power to greatly influence your body image, and your body image has the power to influence your body language.

for you to explore

List different body language behaviors that you believe demonstrate self-confidence.

For example: *sitting up straight, smiling, maintaining eye contact with someone you're talking to*

Your turn:

_____

_____

Now, list different body language behaviors that you believe may come off as overly self-conscious:

For example: *slouching, appearing unhappy, avoiding eye contact*

Your turn:

_____

_____

What are the major differences you notice between the different body language behaviors?

_____

_____

What are some times or situations that you've demonstrated any of the behaviors that you listed above?

_____

_____

How do you think that your body language impacts your body image?

_____

_____

explore more

Below, list some body language behaviors you have that you'd like to improve. Beside each item, write a resolution to stop the behavior. It takes time to change behaviors, so be patient with yourself, and keep practicing until you accomplish your goals.

Body Language Behavior

I twirl my hair a lot.

_____

_____

_____

_____

_____

Resolution

Keep my hands down, but not crossed.

_____

_____

_____

_____

_____

32 use your voice

for you to know

Your voice is a powerful tool. Voicing your thoughts and opinions can increase your self-confidence, which will help improve your body image.

This section covered a lot. You identified your emotional triggers, practiced speaking up and setting healthy boundaries, and learned how your body language impacts your body image and vice versa. It's a lot to take in—and not very easy to work through.

Moving forward, know that there will be times when your opinion isn't popular, but you'll feel heard. There will be times that you want to crawl out of your skin, but you'll have the tools to crawl back in it. There will also be times that your voice shakes and you say the hardest thing imaginable, and when it's over, you'll take a huge sigh of relief and feel so much better. There are perks to using your voice: Like actually eating at the restaurant you want because you told somebody that was where you wanted to go or getting a better grade in a class because you asked for help. Maybe you'll feel an enormous sense of pride when you take a compliment instead of rejecting it. Speaking up will help you feel better about yourself and your body. You deserve that.

for you to explore

Reflect upon the work you just did and write down five things that you want to tell someone. You can look back at the first activity of this section and use some of the things you wrote in your thought bubble. Or, by now, things might be different. It might be something simple. *Mom, I'd like for you to teach me how to make Grandma's lasagna.* Or it might be super difficult. *I don't want to be in a relationship with you anymore.* Perhaps it has something to do with your body. *I need you to stop making comments about my weight when I'm eating.* Or it may have to do with your mind. *Could you please explain our homework again? It's still unclear to me.* Whatever you need to say, write down what it is, who needs to hear it, and when you will say it. Then say it.

What I need to say: _____

_____

Whom I need to say it to: _____

When I will say it by: _____

What I need to say: _____

_____

Whom I need to say it to: _____

When I will say it by: _____

What I need to say: _____

_____

Whom I need to say it to: _____

When I will say it by: _____

What I need to say: _____

_____

Whom I need to say it to: _____

When I will say it by: _____

What I need to say: _____

_____

Whom I need to say it to: _____

When I will say it by: _____

The last seven activities focused on the power of your voice. Use the space below to freewrite your thoughts and hopes and fears and reflections about the activities you completed. What was easy? What was hard? What did you learn? What do you need to work on the most, and how will you do it? What do you wish people knew, and how will you tell them? It can be anything you'd like; it's yours.

_____

_____

_____

_____

_____

_____

_____

_____

Part 5
Moving Forward
(Activities 33–40)

33 life with a healthy body image

for you to know

Can you imagine what your life would be like without an unhealthy relationship with your body? Hopefully by now this seems possible. A healthy body image doesn't mean that each day is filled with body image bliss; it just means that it is balanced, and on most days you generally like your body. Maybe you even love it.

What do you think your life would be like without body image woes?

"I wouldn't worry so much about what other people thought about me."

"I would wear whatever clothes I wanted to."

"I'd go swimming and have fun, like I used to."

"I would stop comparing myself to everyone I see."

"I wouldn't feel the pressure to wear so much makeup."

"I'd be OK with myself."

Those are some pretty strong statements. There is more in store for you than constantly worrying about your body.

for you to explore

Take a moment to think about this question: If you woke up tomorrow morning and your body image issues had magically vanished, what would your life be like? What would be different? How would you know it was different? How would you feel? What would you think about? What behaviors would change? Freewrite your response below.

_____

_____

_____

_____

_____

_____

_____

_____

explore more

Based on your response to the reflection prompts above, choose two things you really want to work on—two things you know you can do. You can definitely choose more if you'd like, but start with at least two. Consider the benefits, drawbacks, and steps you need to take to get yourself there.

For example:

Vanished body image issue: *The belief that nothing looks good on me.*

Benefits: *I wouldn't spend an hour getting ready every morning. I wouldn't wear oversized, baggy clothes all the time (unless I wanted to), and I wouldn't spend my days worried about how I look.*

Drawbacks: *I can't think of any. I hate waking up early and always being late because it takes me forever to get ready.*

Steps to get myself there: *Go through my clothes, get rid of my full-length mirror, and say positive things to myself. Maybe I could also pick out my clothes the night before and commit to wearing them.*

Your turn:

Vanished body image issue: _____

_____

Benefits: _____

_____

Drawbacks: _____

_____

Steps to get myself there: _____

_____

Vanished body image issue: _____

_____

Benefits: _____

_____

Drawbacks: _____

_____

Steps to get myself there: _____

_____

34 body compassion

for you to know

When you have compassion for your body, you treat it with kindness and respect. Having compassion for your body is not dependent on what other people think about you, your grades, how many friends you have, or even what your body looks like. Body compassion is unconditionally accepting your body, as is.

> It's weird to think about being nice to my body all the time. I'm so used to automatically hating it and picking apart my flaws. I read magazines and don't look like the girls in them, I don't get all the attention like my friends do, and I don't always feel great about what I look like. I spend a lot of time saying cruel things to myself. Maybe that's the problem?
>
> —Ginger

The kinder you are to yourself, the healthier your body image will be. It's true. You've done a lot of work throughout this book on replacing negative thoughts and learning to be less judgmental toward your body. Now, let's work on cultivating continuous kindness toward your body.

for you to explore

Read the prompts below, and for each one, write down a real-life example that you have faced. Directly below each statement, use body compassion to reflect how you would now treat your body.

For example:

A time I judged my body: *I'd have more friends if I didn't have this giant hideous scar on my face.*

Body compassion reflection: *My scar tells a story; it is part of me and has nothing to do with how many friends I have. Plus, if someone wants to judge me because of it, they are probably not someone I want to be friends with.*

Your turn:

A time I judged my body: _____

_____

Body compassion reflection: _____

_____

_____

_____

A time somebody else judged my body: _____

_____

Body compassion reflection: _____

_____

_____

_____

A time I blamed my body for something that went wrong: _____

_____

Body compassion reflection: _____

_____

_____

_____

I time I didn't respect my body: _____

_____

Body compassion reflection: _____

_____

_____

_____

A time I felt betrayed by my body: _____

_____

Body compassion reflection: _____

_____

_____

_____

explore more

Part of being compassionate toward your body is giving yourself a break. Think about some things that you want to do, and write yourself a personal permission slip to do them. Then, actually do them.

For example:

I want to go to bed at a reasonable hour and not stay up doing homework until 2:00 a.m.
I want to go to school with messy hair.
I want to say no when my boss asks me to close again on Friday.

Your turn:

Personal Permission Slip

I grant myself permission to

_____

_____

_____

_____

_____

---

for you to know

An affirmation is a little note of positive encouragement. It is a gentle reminder that you are worth it and that things will be OK, even when you think they won't be.

Affirmations support physical, emotional, and spiritual health and boost body confidence. They provide a unique way for you to remind yourself of your good qualities, and redirect, and realign your thoughts along more positive lines.

When I was in middle school, my school counselor used to carry around affirmations in a jar. She would hand them out in the hallway and during lunch. I pretended to be too cool for them, but she always gave me one anyway. I tucked them all away in my backpack and secretly read them later. Before I knew it, my nightstand drawer was full of affirmations! I still have them, and sometimes, when I'm having a bad day, I'll dump the whole drawer out and read them all. They are nice reminders to focus on the good stuff in life.

—Gianna

Creating your own unique affirmations can empower you to let go of the small things and focus on what is important and valuable to you.

for you to explore

There are many ways you can write affirmation statements. You can make a list on a plain piece of paper and cut them out. You can type them up using a fancy font and print them out. You can use index cards and color. Or, you can get artsy and piece together words from newspapers or magazines. If you are having trouble coming up with a mental image of what an affirmation looks like, Google "affirmation cards" to spark your creativity. Some examples of affirmation statements are: *I am worthy. I am lovable. I believe in myself. I am enough. I know how to stay calm. This will be over soon. I enjoy trying new things.* Some affirmation starters are: *I am…, I enjoy…, I love…, I manage…, I create…, I have…, I accept…, I can…, I believe…,* and so on.

Use the space below to draft your affirmations. Try to write at least fifteen. When you are done, transfer them to whatever you choose, and cut them out. You'll make a special place to keep them in the next activity.

1. _____

2. _____

3. _____

4. _____

5. _____

6. _____

7. _____

8. _____

9. _____

10. _____

11. _____

12. _____

13. _____

14. _____

15. _____

explore more

Make a positive-thoughts box to keep your affirmations in. First, you'll need to get
a container to decorate. You can use a shoe box, a tissue box, or a small mailing box.
Next, get some items to use to decorate your box: glue, scissors, tape, writing utensils,
fabric samples, ribbons, stickers, magazines, old photos, or even paint—whatever crafty
materials you'd like. You can design your box however suits you best—it's yours. When
you are done, put all of your affirmations inside and store your box in a special place.
Refer to your affirmations often to remind yourself of the power of positive thinking.

for you to know

We are so connected with technology that it is easy to lose sight of our real-time support system. Interacting with people in real time fuels connection and demonstrates what it's like to have someone truly support you, no matter what.

Think about this: How simple is it to pick up your cell phone and text a friend when you're upset about something? But texting doesn't convey your true feelings and has none of your real voice. It's the same with the Internet; there is no voice. Communicating online isn't a negative thing; it's just important to have people you can talk to in person. Talking to someone in real time will help you feel connected and is a much better way for you to feel heard, understood, and cared for.

Sometimes, when the going gets rough and tough, it may feel like nobody is around. It is important to identify the people in your life you can count on, unconditionally, during these times. And you don't always have to be in some sort of crisis to reach out. The people who unconditionally support you are there whether you're ecstatic or devastated or anything and everything in between. They are the people who care about you and love you, no matter what. Most importantly, they are the people you can be *you* around.

for you to explore

Below, list the people you can count on, in real time, to be there for you. Whether you just need to vent, need help dealing with a friend problem, or are having a major crisis, these are the people you connect with and can count on. These are also the people who will high-five or happily hug you when something fabulous occurs. It is OK if you leave a category blank, and it is OK if you feel like you only have one person you trust and can depend on. It's not the quantity of people; it's the quality.

Family members: _____

Really good friends: _____

Community people (coaches, religious community, teachers, counselor, etc.):

_____

Others: _____

explore more

Now, using your list above, identify the best people to help with your particular needs. Your best friend may be a great listener, but she may not be the right person to give you honest advice. Below, write the name of a person you can count on for each of the prompts. You may have a go-to person who suits every category, or you may have a different person for each need.

The person I can talk to…

When I'm sad: _____

When I just won an award: _____

When I need to vent: _____

When I need to say something really hard: _____

When I need honesty: _____

When I am feeling insecure: _____

When I don't trust myself: _____

When I'm feeling scared: _____

When I need to laugh: _____

When I just need to cry: _____

When I just need a break from reality: _____

When I need advice: _____

When I need someone to hear me: _____

When I need someone to understand me: _____

When I need someone to help me in an emergency: _____

When I just need someone there: _____

What else? Who else? _____

The next time you find yourself in need of a listening ear, refer to your list and reach out for the support you need and deserve. Also, this list can change. Add and delete people as needed—it's your list!

gratitude 37

for you to know

Gratitude means being thankful and showing appreciation for what you have. It focuses on the positive, not the negative. It's being aware of what makes you smile, what makes you thrive, and all the things in life you have to be thankful for.

Gratitude and a healthy body image go hand in hand. You've done numerous activities to help you understand the beauty of what your body does, rather than what it looks like. The simple act of being grateful can help you take a step back and see all the things in your life that are working out well for you. You can show gratitude for the things you may take for granted, like a warm bed and clean clothes. Or you can be grateful for nature, the things that you own, or the important people in your life.

One day I got home from school and needed to quickly change for track practice. I couldn't find the shirt I wanted to wear. I yelled downstairs to my mom asking her where it was. Well, she was washing it. I went crazy. I was screaming at her and acted totally bratty. I grabbed another shirt and stormed out of the house. When I got to practice, I felt really guilty for yelling at her. I mean, she did my laundry, and she couldn't read my mind to know what shirt I wanted to wear. When I got home, I apologized, but she was still really upset with me—not mad, upset. I felt so bad, but I don't blame her. I started thinking about all the things that she does for me and wrote her an apology letter. I have been ultraconscious about thanking her for all the little things now. I have felt better about myself, and we haven't had any fights since. It took that happening to realize I have a lot to be grateful for.

—Maya

When it comes to being grateful, there are no boundaries. There are no rules. You own it; you just have to realize it.

for you to explore

You are going to need a separate piece of paper and something to write with. If you want, use color or cut and paste words from magazines and newspapers. List a hundred things that you are grateful for. Yes, one hundred. This may seem daunting at first, but once you get started it will be easy. Here are a few examples to get you started:

I'm grateful for: *my family, my friends, coffee, cold starry nights, bicycles, books, the Internet, safe water to drink, my health, and my education.*

Now, get your paper and materials and get started! When you are finished, respond to the prompts below:

1. Write down three things you felt while working on this activity.

   _____

   _____

   _____

2. What are you most grateful for? Why?

   _____

   _____

   _____

3. What are some ways that you can continue to show gratitude in your life?

_____

_____

_____

explore more

Create a photo log of what you are grateful for. This may take some time, so don't worry if you cannot do it all at once. Grab your camera or your phone, and try to take a picture of everything on your list. If you cannot physically take a picture of it, take a picture of something that reminds you of it. When you are done, arrange them all in a folder. You can post them on a social media site, make a photo collage, or just have them in a special place to remind you of all you have to be thankful for.

for you to know

There are all sorts of positive benefits to being physically active that have nothing to do with your weight. Engaging in physical activity on a regular basis decreases stress, helps with sleep, promotes healthy bones, increases strength, improves your overall mood, and is a great body image booster.

Whether you are an athlete or someone who absolutely detests exercise, you probably still know it's important to do some sort of physical activity. Here's the caveat: there are so many confusing messages out there saying what you "should" do and how you "should" look as a result. There are too many absurd societal standards that say you must work out to burn calories, lose weight, and get ready for bikini season. These standards are unattainable and miss the entire purpose of being physically active.

The point of this activity is to find ways to move your body that feel good to you. Exercise is about so much more than your weight or the size or shape of your body. Physical activity should be, for the most part, enjoyable. You don't need a fancy gym or a warm climate to move your body. You just need a positive attitude and the motivation to find something that makes you feel great about your mind, body, and spirit. It's fun.

for you to explore

Check out the giant list of ways to be physically active and circle any activities that you currently do, that you enjoy doing, or that you are simply willing to try.

Aerobics	Fishing	Lifting weights	Soccer
Badminton	Football	Martial arts	Softball or baseball
Basketball	Frisbee	Pilates	Stretching
Bowling	Golf	Playing on a playground	Surfing
Boxing/ Kickboxing	Gymnastics	Racquetball	Swimming
Canoeing	Hiking	Rock climbing	Tennis
Cheerleading	Hockey	Rowing	Video games that require you to be active
Childhood games (tag, hopscotch, hide and seek)	Horseback riding	Running	
	Jogging	Skateboarding	Volleyball
	Jumping rope	Skating (roller or ice)	Walking
Cycling	Jumping on a trampoline	Skiing or snowboarding	Yoga
Dancing	Kayaking	Sledding	Zumba
Diving	Lacrosse		Other
Dodgeball			_____

1. Look over your list. Out of everything you circled, what is something that you are willing to commit to that you think you'd enjoy?

_____

2. What activity on the list have you always wanted to try, but for one reason or another, haven't?

_____

3. What stopped you from trying it? For example, your body image, fear of what others might think or say, or your athletic ability.

_____

4. What can you do to overcome what stopped you?

_____

If you are already physically active or participate in an organized sport, write down something else you'd like to try—just for fun.

explore more

Try something you circled in the previous activity and commit to it. Remember that sometimes it takes a while to find what you like to do, and sometimes it takes a while for your body to adjust to something new. Keep at it. Begin by keeping a log of what you do, tracking your moods and the physical feelings of your body.

Exercise I tried: _____

Mood before: _____

Mood after: _____

How my body felt before: _____

How my body felt after: _____

My overall experience was: _____

creating a self-care plan 39

for you to know

As you move forward, it's important to reflect upon the work you've done and to identify ways to take care of yourself and your body. Self-care simply means intentionally caring for your body in a healthy manner. It's prevention. It's also becoming aware of your needs and putting them first in order to be your best self.

Creating a self-care plan, which you'll do in a moment, is a creative way to put yourself in control of how you'll cope with any future body image concerns. You have to determine what areas you might still need to work on, what gentle reminders you may still need, and how you will maintain a positive outlook when things get rough. Self-care involves your mind, body, and spirit.

Here's an example:

Mind: *To calm my mind I like to listen to music, read, or take a really long nap.*

Body: *Taking care of my body means eating healthy foods, exercising, and focusing on what my body can do for me, not just what it looks like.*

Spirit: *To me, my spirit means living in the moment. Sometimes I just have to take a deep breath and remind myself that everything is going to be OK.*

Self-care is a gift you give to yourself. It's listening to your wants, needs, and intuition. When you practice self-care, you are showing your body that you care about and respect it.

for you to explore

Take a moment to ponder how you cope with tough times in your mind, body, and spirit. In the circles below, list the ways you can take care of yourself and your body. Creating this self-care plan will serve as a reminder of all your healthy coping skills.

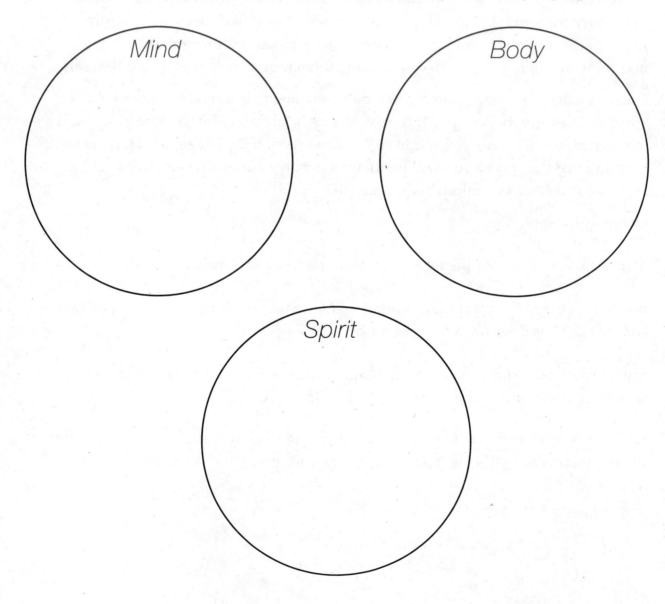

Mind

Body

Spirit

explore more

Based on the skills you have learned while working through this book, write a letter to your future self. First, choose a time frame: three months, six months, two years from now—whatever you wish. Next, using a healthy body image as a focal point, write what you'd like your life to be like in the time frame you chose. You can write about goals, your self-care plan, or your support system. You can give yourself advice, talk about your experiences completing this workbook, or say anything else you'd like to say. When you're done, put the letter in an envelope and write down the date you are going to open it. Put it away in a safe place that you won't forget about and open it on the date you chose.

40 moving forward

for you to know

You're almost finished! Congratulations! You may have reached the end of this workbook, but your journey is just getting started. You can do the activities in this book over and over again, but it's your willingness to move forward that will take you to the next level. Our world is filled with unhealthy messages about what you should and should not look like. You will be bombarded with these messages daily, but hopefully you've learned a lot of skills to fight back and love your body and the skin you're in. Remember: How you feel about your body and how you feel in your body is a choice. You get to make that choice—nobody else does. You have *so much* power.

You've learned all about body image, the pressures of growing up in today's society, how the media affects you, and how you feel about yourself. You've also learned how to confidently use your voice and express your true self and how to treat your body with the love and kindness it wholeheartedly deserves. So, what will you do with all your new self-knowledge? How will you communicate your needs? How will you take care of your body? How will you continue to move forward in a positive direction? The choice is yours.

for you to explore

Think about all the activities in which you've learned about yourself while working on your body image. On the next page, you'll write a body image manifesto. A manifesto is a declaration of intentions and can be very powerful. Begin by flipping through the chapters and noticing the changes you've made. What do you want to keep in mind? What do you need to remind yourself to do? How will you keep moving forward? Declare at least ten ways you will treat your body with the love and respect it deserves.

For example:

I will not insult my body to myself or others.

I will fuel my body with nutritious foods.

Your turn:

My Body Image Manifesto

I will _____

I will _____

I will _____

I will _____

I will _____

I will _____

I will _____

I will _____

I will _____

I will _____

I will _____

I will _____

I will _____

explore more

Journaling can be incredibly cathartic. It will give you a healthy and safe outlet to express your feelings. When you journal, there are no rules, no judgments, and no boundaries—it's just you being yourself. You can write about anything you want in your journal: you can unload whatever is on your mind, you can write your dreams and hopes and goals and plans, you can doodle and draw, or you can make lists—endless lists! To get started, create something that is yours. If you personalize it, you are more likely to use it.

First, you will need a composition notebook, magazines or newspapers, markers, scissors, old books or photos that you can cut up, glue or double-sided tape, and clear packing tape.

Next, decorate the front and back covers of the composition notebook any way you choose. Use a little bit of glue or double-sided tape to secure your decorations.

Then, when you are finished decorating your journal, use the clear packing tape on the front and back covers to keep everything in place.

Finally, just start writing. You're the author of your next story...

*"Take care of your body.
It's the only place you have to live."*

—Jim Rohn

Julia V. Taylor, PhD, is author of *Salvaging Sisterhood* and *Perfectly You*, and is coauthor of *G.I.R.L.S.* (*Girls in Real Life Situations*) and *The Bullying Workbook for Teens*. Taylor has worked as a middle and high school counselor and has a passion for empowering girls to stand up to unrealistic media expectations, take healthy risks, and cultivate meaningful relationships. Visit her online at www.juliavtaylor.com.

Foreword writer **Melissa Atkins Wardy** is the author of *Redefining Girly* and the owner of Pigtail Pals & Ballcap Buddies, an online boutique offering empowering children's apparel. Find her at www.pigtailpals.com.